VIRGIL AND CAESAR

Poetry

Collected Poems 1960–1984

Plays

Agora — a Dramatic Epic,
in chronological order of action
consisting of:

Healing Nature — The Athens of Pericles
Virgil and Caesar
Moving Reflections } The Roman Trilogy
Light Shadows
Byzantium
Living Creation
A Conception of Love
Maquettes for the Requiem   Trilogy of one-act plays
Lying Figures
Killing Time } The Requiem Trilogy
Meeting Ends

Editor

Eleven Poems by Edmund Blunden
Garland
Studies in the Arts

VIRGIL AND CAESAR

a play by Francis Warner

ἀλλ' ἐφ' ὅσον ἐνδέχεται ἀθανατίζειν καὶ πάντα ποιεῖν
πρὸς τὸ ζῆν κατὰ τὸ κράτιστον τῶν ἐν αὐτῷ· εἰ γὰρ καὶ
τῷ ὄγκῳ μικρόν ἐστι, δυνάμει καὶ τιμιότητι πολὺ μᾶλλον
πάντων ὑπερέχει.

Aristotle, *Eth. Nic.* X

OXFORD THEATRE TEXTS 11
COLIN SMYTHE, GERRARDS CROSS, 1993

British Library Cataloguing in Publication Data

Warner, Francis, *1937–*
Virgil and Caesar : a play. — (Oxford Theatre Texts,
ISSN 0141–1152; 11)
1. Title II. Series
822'.914
ISBN 0–86140–348–7

First published in 1993 by Colin Smythe Ltd.,
Gerrards Cross, Buckinghamshire

Distributed in North America by
Dufour Editions, P.O. Box 449, Chester Springs, PA 19425 U.S.A.

'Coast View of Delos with Aeneas' by Claude Lorrain reproduced
by courtesy of the Trustees, The National Gallery, London

Cover design and production photographs by Billett Potter of Oxford

Produced in Great Britain

FOR BENEDICT

All enquiries regarding performing rights should be addressed to the publishers.

VIRGIL AND CAESAR was produced by the Oxford University Dramatic Society (OUDS) for performance in Convocation House, Oxford on Tuesday, February 18th, 1992. The play was sponsored by Adamantios Lemos. The directors were Tim Prentki and Dominic Shellard.

The cast was as follows:

Octavianus Caesar	*Daniel Williams*
Messalla	*Caspar Trenchard*
Agrippa	*Nicholas Poots*
Murena	*Edward Meynell*
Maecenas	*Tim Cunningham*
Virgil	*Mark Payton*
Horace	*Julius D'Silva*
Propertius	*Dominic Shellard*
Herod	*Jason Tann*
Alexander	*David Walters*
Aristobulus	*Ben Beckwith*
Praetorian 1	*David Walters*
Praetorian 2	*Ben Beckwith*
Livia	*Sophie Paul*
Julia	*Alice Kennedy*
Terentia	*Susanna Kane*

Lighting David Colmer. Electrician James Strachan. Costumes Penelope Warner with the Royal Shakespeare Company, Royal National Theatre, Bradfield College and Wendy MacWherter. Make-up Jennifer Davis. Production Assistant and Props Katherine Weir. Stewards Dawn Akers, Pamela Merritt, Kevin Payne, Paul Speaker, Shawn Stogsdill, Johanna Telke, Jean Terry, Neal Wise. Assistant Director James Strachan. OUDS President Tim Cunningham.

Characters

Octavianus Caesar	*afterwards* Augustus Caesar
Messalla	*an aristocrat*
Agrippa	*a General*
Murena	*a Barrister and General*
Maecenas	*Adviser to Caesar, Patron*
Virgil	*Poet*
Horace	*Poet*
Propertius	*Poet*
Herod	*King of Judaea*
Alexander	*Son of Herod*
Aristobulus	*Son of Herod*
First Praetorian Guard	
Second Praetorian Guard	
Livia	*Wife of Caesar, afterwards* Augusta
Julia	*Daughter of Caesar*
Terentia	*Wife of Maecenas*

The play opens in 29 B.C. and ends in 19 B.C.

Act One: Rome.   Act Two: Rome and Brundisium.

Act One

MESSALLA *and* AGRIPPA.

MESSALLA Egypt has fallen. Cleopatra's dead,
Although her effigy in gold, in death,
Held high, enthroned, compels all eyes. Her children,
Selene Cleopatra, and Helios,
Young Moon and Sun, her twins by Antony,
Follow in Caesar's triumph, captured spoil.
Look! Here they weep through the triumphal arch
Swaying to Venus' temple. Last of all,
Leading the Consul and the Senators,
The golden chariot rides the Sacred Way
In which a young god stands, a living flame
Fanned by the crowd's emotion, till his heat
Purifies, fuses and transmutes all Rome.
With victor's laurel crowned, Octavian
At thirty-three is master of the world.

AGRIPPA Today's the third day of Octavian's triumph:
Dalmatia, Actium, now Egypt sprawls.
We have paraded quite enough for me.
There go the cattle for the sacrifice.
Messalla, how was that cow trapped on land?

MESSALLA The Queen? Oh, you were otherwise engaged,
Leading our fleet, Agrippa: four hundred ships—
With catapults you had invented . . .

AGRIPPA   Yes,
For firing grapnels. Antony's flagship
Was clutched, but he jumped to another, followed
Cleopatra. His poor fighting men,
Abandoned, hungry, beaten on land, girl-led,

Changed sides: dined with our welcoming
    legions. She?

MESSALLA   Proculeius told her Caesar's terms,
And she gave hers. She spoke through a little
    grating.
Next day, when he returned with Rome's reply,
Gallus came with him; and, while Gallus talked,
Proculeius climbed in at the window.
She tried to stab herself. You know the rest.

AGRIPPA   You were proscribed, a price set on your head
By this Octavian thirteen years ago:
And yet, when he was helpless, in despair,
Broken by Pompey, his whole fleet shrunk to
An armour-bearer in a rowing boat,
You cherished and restored him, sending news
Along the mountain to Abala's strand
That cheered us all to trumpet: 'Caesar's safe!'

MESSALLA   You, who were with me in the ships at Mylae,
Remember? For him I left Antony
When Cleopatra's clouds absorbed his sky
And drained his light till he became her slave.
I blew his embers, but the flame was dark.

AGRIPPA   Aristocratic Roman, you embody
Magnanimity, which I admire;
But a plebeian background made me stubborn.
Victory was enough at Naulochus
For me. No celebration; no acclaim.

MESSALLA   Our relaxation's over. Caesar comes
To wash, like us, and dust off all the shouts.
Exhilaration and serenity
Strangely combine in him.

AGRIPPA   We were young friends.
I sailed with him to Apollonia
At the command of Julius Caesar, who
Had just made him his heir. We were eighteen.

Rufus came with us. Legionaries taught
Us how to kill, and heal—dark trades—to train
For Parthian campaigns.

PRAETORIAN 1   The victor comes!

PRAETORIAN 2   Messalla and Agrippa, guard him well.

SCENE TWO

Enter OCTAVIANUS CAESAR.

CAESAR   Great tasks require great helpers. Those who
                    serve
              The state deserve high rank. My own true
                    friends.
              Messalla, brother Consuls as we were
              At Actium, for your strong loyalty
              I shall create you Prefect of all Rome —
              To discipline the slaves and keep the peace.

MESSALLA   Triumphant Caesar, many and not unearned
              Are the rewards Rome showers on her sons.
              You have transplanted enemies into friends,
              Grafting their expertise to Caesar's kiss,
              And blushed blood into milk as no man has.
              When I am old, beside my stream, and white
              Narcissi edge their scent with timid crimson
              Where long-stemmed cowslips by the primrose
                    slope
              Vary their dapple under dangling vines
              While a light poplar overbends my cave,
              I shall recall the flame beneath the flowers
              That was young Caesar; how Mount Etna burst
              Sparking the snows, when Julius Caesar fell,
              To bring his great inheritor to power.

CAESAR   You stole soft hours of poetry from Law
              To be with Virgil when rich Philodemus

Taught him beside the Bay of Luxury.
Now you've a group of poets—Tibullus,
Lygdamus, and your niece Sulpicia,
Even as Maecenas nurtures now for me
Mild Virgil, Horace, and our urban boy
Propertius—he must avoid affectation!
When Mars and today's triumph are full filled
No better calm can coming evenings bring
Than words sung to the lyre; perhaps a play
By Aristophanes, or Eupolis.
My deputy, Agrippa, you who won
The crown, woven in gold of prows of ships,
For victory at Naulochus, receive
Later today an azure flag, your ensign,
In honour of your Actium victory.

AGRIPPA   Great Caesar, thanks. I lack Messalla's breeding
And oratory, but I'm Roman stock.
In me the ideal of service does not change.
When Hannibal of Carthage (as a boy
Pledged by his father to hatred of Rome)
In coalition with the outer tribes—
African, Gallic, Spanish, who knows else—
Well-financed by Philip of Macedon,
Stabbed sixty thousand of our Roman boys
At Cannae in one day, he did not win.
The coalition soon dissolved. At Zama,
Stripped of her conquests, bankrupt, allyless,
Carthage renounced her role as superpower.
Let me remind you, in your days of glory,
Spanish and African must be subdued.

CAESAR   Agrippa, you are right. Yes. I will go
From Burgos, over the Cantabrian mountains,
And with three columns impose peace on
      Spain.

AGRIPPA   I shall go with you.

CAESAR   Next year you will be
Consul, with me—and we must purge the Senate,

Grown far too big with idlers uninvolved—
So Rome will need you while I am away.
Then I'll become a private citizen,
And hand all power back, where it belongs,
Freely to the Senate and People of Rome.
The cavalcade moves on. Friends! At my sides.
The red god Mars has now made Rome
    supreme.
Our shrine of Venus holds the golden queen.

Exeunt.

SCENE THREE

JULIA *dressing* LIVIA*'s hair;* TERENTIA *attending.*

LIVIA   Make my hair perfect for the Triumph Feast
Tonight, girls.

JULIA   Mother, how would Father like it?

LIVIA   Not the old fashion, Julia—wavy bandeaux
Holding the chignon low on the nape of the
    neck,
Heavy and hot, a cushion of hair on the
    forehead.
That's fine for Caesar's sister, not his wife.
What I now like is: small flat ripples of hair
Growing to deep waves, iron-hot; tiny curls
Flirting and glimpsing out from under the
    bandeaux.
I may be twenty-nine . . .

JULIA   But Caesar's wife
In triumph! I'm so proud of both of you.
Cleopatra, they say, wrote a book
On coiffures and cosmetics. Terentia,
You do your husband's hair in waves. Maecenas
Uses the curling tongs, I'm sure—strokes myrrh

Into his ringlets to waft scent. Help me.
Is it true he feeds guests young donkey meat?

TERENTIA   I've still so much to learn about his ways.
You know we're newly married, and he's lived
Three times as long as I have. Forty-five!
Some friends of his I like—the poets, Virgil,
And Horace; but his ballet-dancer friend,
Bathyllus, hates me.

JULIA   Jealous, I suppose.
Maecenas has all the gifts—wealth, a young
          wife.
He is descended from Etruscan kings;
The perfect diplomat; yet he still wears
His tunic with only a narrow stripe,
Not the broad purple band Senators flaunt.

TERENTIA   He says honours imprison and stifle. Now
He's free to choose his friends. Will you be, too,
When you are married to Marcellus?

JULIA   He's
Only a little older than myself;
I'll shape his tastes to my fun. What's that,
          Mother?
(*Aside to* TERENTIA) She's my step-mother. Father
          married her
When he was twenty-four and she nineteen,
Married already, pregnant by her first husband!
'The lucky have children in three months,'
          Rome said.
I'm a young girl; but I've been twice engaged.
Why, many marry at twelve! Yes; I like men.
That sting-tongued soldier-barrister and wit
Your half-brother, Murena; he's ambitious.
Look at Agrippa's shoulders! Don't you feel
His hands rubbing your back, your willing slave?

TERENTIA   One in two wives of slaves and freedmen die
By thirty; most of these by twenty-five.

That's why your father wants this marriage-law
Fining all women childless at twenty;
Men, twenty-five.

JULIA   The birthrate feeds the legions.
If (all the gods forbid!) my father died,
Marcellus might be heir! Queen I would sit,
Terentia: sole lady of the world.
How can we keep our husbands in our power?

LIVIA   You prattle! Rome loathes kings—and queens.
           From me
Take some advice: please him with all your guiles.
Help each ambition. Be discreet. Don't see
When a new favourite strokes his arm and smiles.
Medusa jealousy will petrify
All tenderness from marriage. Still your tongue.
Lives, nations may depend on your blind eye,
And strong men sometimes need to be kept
          young.

JULIA   Your generosity's self-interest.
Now, while that dries, I've asked—if you don't
          mind—
Propertius up to sing, as you are dressed,
The ideal Roman woman he's defined.

LIVIA   Then bring him in. Cicadas and the dusk
Must be his harmony, heavy as musk.

SCENE FOUR

Enter PROPERTIUS.

PROPERTIUS   Wearing the Muses' altar-gown
          I come, your poet-priest,
Offer a calf and ivy-crown,
          Libations for the feast
Of Caesar's glory. May all harms

Leave for a distant sky:
I sing of the whole world in arms,
    And Roman victory.

And here at home call from the grave
    Cornelia, Paullus' wife.
'Whose tears water the flowers that wave
    Above my afterlife?
No prayers call back the ferryman,
    No matter how august.
Darkness is now my guardian,
    Five fingers hold my dust.

My innocence was yours alone,
    Paullus. From wedding flame
To funeral brand and unburned bone
    No accusations shame.
My house was noble. Nature gave
    Me laws which I obeyed.
Married to one alone, I'm brave
    To meet Dis unafraid.

Now you must play the mother's part,
    Loved husband left behind;
And when you grieve, conceal the smart;
    Kiss their tears, and be kind.
Yes, kiss them twice, from me. At night
    When worn with dreams you lie
Lonely, imagine, by your light,
    My picture makes reply.

If he should marry, children, speak
    Well of your father's choice,
And do not tell her I'm unique.
    Welcome her, and rejoice!
If he should face old age alone
    Content with only me,
Save him from sorrow when you're grown.
    My lost years may he see.'

SCENE FIVE

MURENA, HORACE *and* VIRGIL *have entered.*
LIVIA, JULIA *and* TERENTIA *have left.*

MURENA   All the old values of the white-haired days.

PROPERTIUS   Thank you, Murena.

MURENA   Yes, the Roman wife.

HORACE   Propertius, your Cornelia deflects
                Actium's praise. You prefer women to war
                Again. Your battlefield's the narrow bed
                Where pinioned thighs shudder at clash of
                        arms.

PROPERTIUS   Horace, a pair of girls claimed me their guest
                As I could best reign at their banquet of curls.
                No son of mine shall live by taking life.
                I mourned my father in Perugia
                (Rome massacred Italians in that war)
                And gathered, far too young, his blood-hacked
                        bones,
                While our lush farms were snatched for
                        soldiers' pay:
                Virgil's farm, too—though Virgil's poems won
                Octavius Caesar's clemency, and gift
                Of new land, south of Rome, on the Greek
                        Crater,
                Where from Misenum to Minerva's cape
                House touches garden, garden touches house,
                Till the whole gulf's a single bowl of fruit.
                Yet, even so, it's Caesar's camp I'll follow.
                Let the young poets sing of love; when old
                Praise war, when woman's touch no longer stirs.

HORACE   Like you, I lost my father and our land;
                Dropped my dishonoured sword at Philippi,

With Brutus fought against Octavian,
Philippi's victor, who—generously wise—
Welcomed opposing troops in amnesty.
Those days search for oblivion.

MURENA   Not from me!
Caesar's a sick man, and buys acquiescence.
Didn't Maecenas give you your estate,
Horace, among unbroken Sabine hills,
Lulled by your endlessly chattering crystal
       spring?
No neighbours? Yours the only level ground?
Maecenas gives what others lost. Yet I
Have done the same. For Caesar I suppressed
The arrogant Salassi who blocked the Alps;
Slaughtered until they knelt, then sold those
       left—
Some forty-thousand—as twenty-year slaves
On market days at Eporedia.
Their land I gave to our Praetorians.

VIRGIL   Was it your will, Jupiter, we who are
To live in peace should tear ourselves in war?

PROPERTIUS   Yesterday's garlands, let them be my pillow
As fits a poet of love. If all men lay
As I do, warm with wine, no bones would drift
Tossed beneath Actium's waves. Let Virgil sing
Of Actium's shore watched by sun-bright Apollo,
And marvelling ships of Caesar. Virgil writes
Of how Aeneas came from Troy to Rome
Founding the walls we honour to this day.
Stand aside, Greeks! Writers of Rome, give way!
A greater than the *Iliad* is born!

Enter MAECENAS.

MAECENAS   My poets, you may knock my teeth out, hunch
My back, sever the muscles to my feet,
My hips, my hands, impale me on a spit—
But if one spark of life is left in me,

Cherish it. Yes. That's my philosophy.
Octavian comes. Which of you is to sing
The Actium victory?

PROPERTIUS   If Fates had been
Generous enough to endow me with arts
Appropriate, Maecenas, I would praise
The skills and wars of your Caesar, his triumphs,
The beaks of ships along the Sacred Way.
But I will welcome chariots of booty
Lying between my girl-friend's breasts, reading
Aloud the names of captured cities, stare
At snorting horses shying from the shouts
At captured kings flung down beneath their
      shields.

MAECENAS   Am I a ship rolling without ballast?

VIRGIL   Night's showers turn down the sky, spread out
      in stars,
And drowsy creatures of the fields crawl home;
Colours withdraw, and rustling lives fall still.
What I can do to honour him, I will.

SCENE SIX

Enter CAESAR.

CAESAR   Maecenas, how can I face my pile of letters?
You know my life, and health. I used to cope.
Would Horace be my secretary scribe?
Personal matters only: he's discreet.
From your table of parasites he'll be
Regally fed at mine.

MAECENAS   Ah, Caesar, you
Are able to persuade. Look after him
As you would me. Horace, what do you say?

HORACE   You shoulder, every day, the entire world,

Protecting all, guiding our laws, our morals—
Great Caesar, who am I to claim your thoughts?
In your own lifetime we acknowledge you
Superhuman, with altars, vows, and praise.
We poets are our own worst enemies.
When asked to sing, nothing will make us. When
Neglected, there's no way to silence us.

CAESAR   Your name came up in conversation. Ask
Septimius what I said. I'm not too pleased.
The reason is I do not find my name
In your new book; among recipients
Of those fine verse epistles. They are good!
Write more. Is it that you're embarrassed that
Posterity might mock you as my friend?
Since you decline my intimacy, note:
We do not haughty-toitinize in pique.
Use my home as if you were my household;
Take what you need; and, if your health allows,
Share me some hours from your immortal
            poems.

Exit HORACE.

Livia tells me that you sang to her
Of Actium's waves and my Cornelia's death.
What of that scamp Cynthia, and your girls?

PROPERTIUS   Cynthia was first, Cynthia shall be the last.
God Caesar, I intend to celebrate
Brave men in battle and my leader's camp.
Praise me for daring, if not for what comes.

MAECENAS   Oh do, Propertius. It would be a change
From lamplit sprawls and unknown references.

PROPERTIUS   Maecenas, you Etruscan prince, why launch
Me on so vast an ocean for my pen?
Set an example! Your lines can pace mine,
And your name, too, will shape the lips of Time.
Mighty Caesar, Caesar mighty in war,

In love, defeated nations do not score.

Exit PROPERTIUS.

CAESAR He's too divided to succeed beyond
Records of pillow-pressing. Keep my name
Out of all poets' books, except the serious.
Murena, I admire with gratitude
All you have done to keep the Alpine pass
To Gaul and Upper Rhine free for the troops
And trade; but in the court you cross-examine
With a sardonic insolence and wit
That's all the limited outlook of a dentist.

MURENA I merely asked: 'What are *you* doing here?
Who summoned you?'

CAESAR   And I replied: 'The State.'
Well, barristers must probe. Your sister proves
A good wife, Maecenas?

MAECENAS   What's mine is yours.

Exeunt MAECENAS *and* MURENA.

SCENE SEVEN

CAESAR At last, my Virgil; you and I alone
For a few moments before Herod comes.
I need your company as I did when,
A boy of fifteen, I looked up to you,
My senior fellow-student, in the lectures
Of dry Epidius, who taught us both.

VIRGIL And taught Mark Antony the endless curbs
And bombast of the Asianic style,
Those empty colour-flasks of rhetoric . . .

CAESAR I've kept a note you pushed along in class:

'Enough of futile rules by greasy pedants.
Let's spread our sails for a far wiser don,
Siro the Epicurean, and be free.'

VIRGIL   Octavian, I—from a northern province—
Came late to learning. You, who at the grave
Of Julius Caesar's sister, your grandmother,
Gave the laudation when you were just twelve,
Winning the admiration and the love
Of Julius Caesar; his adoption, too,
As heir; you were already confident
In public speaking. Your high birth shone out.
Men and boys flocked like sparrows to the
        plough
To ride or walk with you. Your looks disturbed
Admiring women so much, on feast days
Your mother made you worship after dusk.

CAESAR   Yet you were patient with me, through all praise,
And gave me your first poem—on a gnat!
'Like tiny spiders, we've spun our slight
        thread . . .'

VIRGIL   You still remember!

CAESAR   You were six years older
Than I; are infinitely wiser, still.
Why did you make me think of Antony?
Ambition's thrust and honour's scaly tail
Compelled me to destroy that brother-in-law,
Once my true friend-in-arms, then enemy.
War brings out values that the cynical—
Propertius—lightly dismiss and call naive:
Loyalty, heroism, patience,
True, noble selflessness when, at the crucial
Moment, life's gambled.

VIRGIL   Magnanimity,
Especially to prisoners and defeated.

CAESAR   Yes. Best of all—reliability,

Agrippa's gift, without which, peace—our aim,
The point of all our pain—disintegrates.

VIRGIL   Survival means there are times when we kill;
                Yet we must still respect—even a wasp—
                What dies, and realize what's being done:
                Make the death brief, decisive, with least fear
                And pain. How much more if a man?

CAESAR   Virgil,
                You never give us the triumphal shout.

VIRGIL   Enough we win. Yes. As the severed hand
                Slacks and clutches its sword-grip, gropes for its
                        owner
                Whose drumming heels on the hard, blood-
                        soaked earth
                A life breathes into breeze, perhaps the gods
                Grieve at our suffering.

CAESAR   I know you're right.
                Oh, Antony! In younger battles he
                Was like a high wind in the Cyclades,
                When even the stubborn fig and olive trunks
                Hunch and bow down while vines are stripped
                        of grapes,
                Turning peace, like a sea of glass, into
                Sea-horses curling wavy manes far out
                To the horizon, while the frightened sand
                Pulls from the clawing ranks its sifting gold.
                He fell in love with his past youth, grappled
                By Egypt's perfumed bait; sat in her ship,
                General no more, his head sunk in his hands:
                A ladybird that clings a leaf in storm.
                Let it be you who sings of Actium
                And writes my epic for posterity.

VIRGIL   After the battle, Caesar, when you paused
                And, at Atella with Maecenas, we
                Rested, we read my *Georgics* to you. There
                I sang the skull-chipped swords of Philippi

With rusty helmets that a farmer digs
Up with his hoe and curved plough till he
    stares,
Bent over, at large bones in upturned graves.
If I'm to sing how you subdued the world,
I'll carve in gold on doors of ivory,
Where circling dolphins plunge, the surging
    Nile
In the full flood of war, our greatest Caesar
Leading the men of Mars and Italy,
Your Father's comet shining from your brow.
Towering Agrippa heads this line of ships
Crowned with his woven victory. Here strong
Antony, with natives of the dawn
And—yes, the shame of it—Egyptian wife,
Barks with Anubis and her crocodiles
Against our Neptune, Venus, Minerva.
Now the whole ocean, lashed by pulling oars,
Incarnadines the runnels of the deep.
Caesar, I'll build a temple in my verse,
I'll offer gifts as priest, with olive crowned,
But do not ask me ever to forget
A father's groan of anger as he's killed.

SCENE EIGHT

Enter MAECENAS.

MAECENAS   Each of you is immortal. You need time
Simply together.

CAESAR   But I see my time
With private friends, like the last raindrops on
The basking branches, is claimed by the day.
You come to tell me Herod waits outside?

MAECENAS   The master of the world need never charm
An Idumaean client-king of Jews.
Why! Let him wait a week.

CAESAR   Not courteous.
Waiting's a beggar that distracts all thought
Down to anticipation's greasy cap;
And restless worry toothaches concentration.
Send in Judaea's king to feel my thoughts.
Bring me Vipsanius Agrippa, and Messalla.

Exit MAECENAS.

Virgil, each nation's customs are cement,
Provided they do not conflict with Rome.
I do not like to be addressed as god,
And the Jews know, as well as we do, that
The Most High God must be invisible,
Behind all nature and above all stars.
Inside their Temple at Jerusalem
They let no visible statue of the god,
No man-made emblem, enter; I respect
The one place in the world where the Unseen,
Holy not through fear or power, but good,
The Name above all Names, is glorified
Within their consecrated sanctuary.

Exit VIRGIL.

Enter MESSALLA *and* MAECENAS.

Messalla and Maecenas, tell me what
Options have I, if I execute
This friend of Cassius and Antony?
Is royal Hyrcanus, whose life has seen
Wide suffering, in his old age our man?

MESSALLA   His is the royal blood, not Herod's; but
A seventy-year-old High Priest can scarcely
Honour Rome long—yet Julius Caesar loved
Hyrcanus, spared him tribute to rebuild
The bees'-gold walls of high Jerusalem.

MAECENAS   There is a problem. When this princely priest
Gave Herod his grand-daughter Mariammë

To be his Hasmonaean bride, and lust,
And came, against advice, to bless their nuptials,
This homesick exile and last royal male,
Mild Hyrcanus, improperly, was strangled.

CAESAR   What kind of son-in-law becomes a traitor?
East of the Hellespont three provinces—
Asia, Bithynia and Syria—
Wall our protection from barbarian spears.
Nearer, Amyntas the Galatian,
Who came to our side at Philippi, rules
From ship-strewn Halys to Pamphylia . . .

MESSALLA   Since Herod's ship docked at Brundisium,
He has not pranced his diadem, nor glowed
In orient silk on Ophir's almug wheels
With apes and peacocks of the ivory East,
But, like a Roman commoner, he walks,
Dignified, with the spirit of a king,
Bareheaded. Unperfumed, he waits your word.

MAECENAS   Messalla's right. No-one can extract tax
And Roman tribute for us as can Herod.

CAESAR   I'll judge him for myself. Agrippa! Come.

SCENE NINE

Enter AGRIPPA, *behind him* HEROD *with* MURENA.

CAESAR   A word, Agrippa. (*Aside*) Did Cassius and Brutus
                    make
Herod the guardian of the fortresses
And armaments?

AGRIPPA   Prefect of Syria
With horse and troops at his disposal.

CAESAR   What

Do the Jews think?

AGRIPPA   That he is cruel, but lucky.

CAESAR   King Herod, I have made you risk the waves
              To stand before me so you can explain
              On one hand your support of Antony
              Against us; on the other, your good help
              To Quintus Didius, intercepting Antony's
              Gladiators summoned by his queen
              From Cyzicus and Trapezus.

HEROD   Mighty Caesar, as I walked through Rome
              And saw the Forum, centre of the world,
              And on the rostra—the high platform where
              Antony spoke your father's funeral speech—
              Among the bronze prows of the Latin ships
              Captured at Actium, I saw—now shrivelled—
              The severed hands and head of Cicero,
              I knew you would not tolerate excuse.

CAESAR   Cicero was a lover of his country,
              A man of eloquence.

HEROD   Yet you acquiesced
              In his death by Antony's agents.

CAESAR   Yes.

HEROD   I have no eloquence, no rhetoric,
              Only bare truth. Antony made me king,
              And I was grateful out of loyalty.
              Had not Arabia beckoned out my sword
              I should have fought with him at Actium.
              As it was, I sent grain, such men as could
              Be spared to fight—for what is friendship if
              Not a response when generous friends cry out
              For help? Nor, after Actium, did I fail
              To give him all the best advice I knew.
              If he'd kill Cleopatra, I had wealth,
              An army, secure walls, I'd be beside him

To save, protect, and re-establish love
Between you, keep power, unite childhood
    friends.
His face lay in her lap. Besotted, he
Threw away all tomorrows from her knee.
His folly was your fortune. Passion's corpse,
Who had outshone the marbled pyramids.
Actium's Apollo granted you his queen,
His death, the treasure of the Ptolemies.
My crime was loyal friendship. With his fall
I here lay down my conquered diadem.

CAESAR   Can you transfer that selflessness to those
More fortunate?

HEROD   The ideal does not change
With the changed name of benefactor-friend.
My safety rests on my integrity.

Pause.

CAESAR   Take up the diadem. I here restore
Your kingdom to you with a Caesar's touch;
Also the lands that Cleopatra seized
Through Antony: your balsam gardens, palms
Of Jericho, and gums of the Dead Sea—
All Palestine except for Ascalon.

HEROD   Caesar, whenever Rome shall need my help—
Whether to quell the Jewish provinces,
Or throw Italy's enemies to dogs—
I shall be loyal to you, yes, and freely
Liberal to your legions, water them
Sun-parched through sand-dunes, and will
    never fail.

CAESAR   Antony's folly has bequeathed you to us,
And gratitude is proved by probing Time.

HEROD   Great Caesar, in whose open palm I live:
May I ask one request? Alexas' life?

He was a friend of Antony. He begs
For mercy.

CAESAR   No! He is anathema,
And I am under oath! He dies. But you
Who suffered Cleopatra's land-greed, take
A gift: her bodyguard, four hundred Gauls;
And for your Jewish Temple I endow
A bull and two lambs to be sacrificed
Each day to God, from me.

HEROD   That will help me, too, with the Sanhedrin—
Or Synedrion as I call it, now
It's stripped and tamed.

CAESAR   The fluent tutor to
Cleopatra's children shall be yours.

HEROD   Nicolas of Damascus!

CAESAR   You may go.
Gifts for your princess Mariammë will
Go with you, and when next I travel East
Through Syria to Egypt, I'll review
Your troops with you at Ptolemaïs.

HEROD   Caesar.

Exit HEROD.

SCENE TEN

MURENA   Couldn't we just exterminate the Jews,
Like the Salassi?

MAECENAS   Herod's doing that
Already.

MURENA   Cicero said the Jews conspired

Against the finest Romans.

CAESAR   That remark
Taught them to side with Julius Caesar, and
My father gave them as reward freedom
From military service, their own courts,
Licence to live in their communities,
And, above all, the worship of their God.
Those synagogues do not disturb Rome's peace
But inculcate the moral decencies—
Justice, and reverence. Encourage them!
Send on their gifts and contributions to
Their holy Temple at Jerusalem!
And when the monthly cash grants, and the food
Bounties our other citizens enjoy
Happen to fall on their strict Sabbath day,
Set theirs aside until the sun goes down.

MURENA   The Roman legal system since the Twelve
Tables has been discipline enough
To make Rome mighty. Are the Jews depraved
That they need more? Why must the Jewish Law
Be cherished like a boil in the state?
What makes them different?

AGRIPPA   The Jews fight well
For abstract nouns; and they are far more strict.
Herod's not a true Jew, and knows it: he
Wants to bring Judaea into our new world,
Hellenize it—not Hebrew coinage: Greek;
And boldly builds an amphitheatre
Where condemned men hand-fight with
                strangest beasts—
To the Jews rank impiety; to us
Matinée entertainment. Caesar, I'll need
His help in Pontus on the Bosphorus
If we replace that mad usurper with
Our Pontic King of Cappadocia.

MAECENAS   I wish he'd brought his spices in with him.

MESSALLA   When I remember I, who overran

Your camp at Philippi, am now your friend,
And see how from the fangs of this new war
You play the syrinx and a cobra waves
In spellbound admiration as he leaves,
Diplomacy, I learn, is about pride,
As economics is psychology.
Octavian, you are father of us all,
And time will rightly praise you as 'August'.

CAESAR   In, to the banquet, show him Roman cheer!
I'll join you shortly. See, my wife is here.

Exeunt.

SCENE ELEVEN

Enter LIVIA.

LIVIA   Husband, today's the anniversary
Of that small boy who might have been our son
Had he not been so anxious to intrude
Into our weeping world three months too soon.
I often think about him.

CAESAR   My Livia.

LIVIA   How infinitely precious is a life!
You've taught me more than I can ever know;
And though our women's intellects are weak,
And, men say, cannot grasp a concept, just
Physical objects through the body's sense,
Yet you have shown me what the Greeks taught
    you:
That all our living world is made of shadows
Thrown by ideas in a far distant realm
Which only by pure reason can be seen—
And the supreme idea is Goodness.

CAESAR   Yes.

Goodness created all; Authority
Controls what is created; and the two
Are made one by the Logos, inward thought,
Conceived in Goodness by Authority.

LIVIA

The sun burns self-sufficient in the sky,
It needs no fuel; yet all light and life
Spring from its influence upon our world.
Goodness exists, and causes to exist.
I feel the Jews know this. So, if I may,
Those golden cups and bowls that would have
　　　welcomed
Our shadow, I'll send to Jerusalem
Where, in the Temple, they may sanctify
The memory of our lost only child.

CAESAR

What better place? Yes. Virgil's lines ring true:
'O Father, O unending power who rules
Men, and all things, how could there ever be
Another we implored to hear our prayers?'
Leave now, and I will wipe away your tears.

Exeunt.

SCENE TWELVE

JULIA *and* PROPERTIUS.

JULIA

Your poem pleased my step-mother, Propertius;
But I must hear what Cynthia does with you.

PROPERTIUS

Julia, what would happen if your father,
Who's trying to make adultery a crime,
And force all bachelors to marry, heard
Me telling you, his daughter, Cynthia's pranks?

JULIA

His life's not blameless—and, I'm getting
　　　married!
Marcellus is absorbed preparing a

Spectacular entertainment as the Senate
Grooms him for post of Aedile. He may be
Consul ten years under the usual age.
I'll make him pay attention to me with
The tricks I'll show him Cynthia taught you.
You heard that law . . ?

PROPERTIUS   Bachelor-tax repealed
Today! Which I could not have paid. She wept,
I cried, when we believed it parted us
(Not even Jove can separate true lovers)
And I, a married husband, might pass by
Her locked doors with an anguished backward
    glance
At the way in so often I'd betrayed;
Or pass her window worn with midnight rope
Down which she'd dangle, hand over hand, to
    reach
My outstretched arms, and there in the road
    not wait
But warm the ground with passion, breasts on
    breast.

JULIA   Can married love be just as passionate?

PROPERTIUS   Marcellus is Augustus' cheerful nephew,
The prince, of every Roman matron's dreams,
That mothers long to have as son-in-law.
He will replace as Caesar's nearest prop
Agrippa . . .

JULIA   Whom I fancy.

PROPERTIUS   Do you? He's
Married to Augustus' niece, Marcellus' sister
Marcella, so you are kin and you may kiss.
Though I can't marry Cynthia, our wild year
Of frenzy has not flagged. The only man
To find life's bliss with just one girl is he
Whose heart is never unattached, never free.
Let great Agrippa build your aqueduct

The Aqua Julia at his own expense
And scatter Rome with fountains, marble bowls,
Till free baths wash both men and women,
     strengthen
The cleaned-out drains till gaping Romans see
     him
Sail through them underground into the Tiber.
Let him rain haircuts, salt, and olive oil,
Theatre tickets; ban astrologers;
Pay for the pampered children of the Senate
To weave and gallop in that old Troy Game.
Let his munificence enhance us all
As he wins every battle that he fights—
Always for Caesar, never for himself;
I'll build my immortality in verse;
As slaves shake dying torches' embers bright,
With daylight creep in Cynthia's stolen bed.

SCENE THIRTEEN

Enter VIRGIL *and* MURENA.

VIRGIL   Julia, your father wants to talk to you.

JULIA   About the wedding! Not the way you do,
                Propertius. I've enjoyed your anecdotes.
                May I meet Cynthia?

PROPERTIUS   If you want disaster.
                Let each keep to their loved one, even when
                Familiar boredoms nudge to something new.
                If you ignore my warning, ah! too late
                These words will echo round your rueful pate.

                Exit JULIA.

VIRGIL   You breathe her young imagination warm.

MURENA   Come, warm us, too!

PROPERTIUS   Happily, but not now.
                 Haven't you news for me? Not about Cynthia!

MURENA   I have, and we need leisure to discuss
                 Someone more serious than her.

PROPERTIUS   With me?

MURENA   I've been defending Primus, our Proconsul
                 Of Macedonia, in court; accused
                 Of making war without authority
                 On Thrace, the Odrysae.

VIRGIL   Did he?

MURENA   He did
                 Make war, but says Octavian told him to.
                 Marcellus, also.

VIRGIL   Why the trial?

MURENA   Caesar
                 Appeared in court himself, and when the
                          Praetor
                 Asked if he'd sent instructions, he said: 'No.'

VIRGIL   Caesar should know! What was the verdict?

MURENA   Many
                 Voted to acquit Primus, but with that word
                 'No' the defence collapsed. Condemned to die.
                 Why is Rome supine under this man's word?
                 We banished kings with Tarquin. Now the scales
                 Of justice tip from health to death by one
                 Breath of Octavian.

VIRGIL   There was a free vote
                 You say?

MURENA   Yes; but his influence is such
                 No vote is free when hangers-on want much.

Virgil, I need to speak to him alone.
I'll see you shortly by Octavian's throne.

Exit VIRGIL.

SCENE FOURTEEN

PROPERTIUS   What do you want of me?

MURENA   Your hand-cupped ear.
Fannius Caepio will not watch a man
Like Primus, decent Governor of a province
The size and dignity of Macedonia,
Fall to authority of one man's whim.
Where is the liberty we praise Rome for?
The old Republican ideals?

PROPERTIUS   Murena,
You'll never make a Cassius. Guard your tongue.

MURENA   Are our tongues locked by Caesar's Actium key?
May we not shout when our rights are curtailed?
We are not horses broken by a god
But men of Rome who think, debate, and vote
Equally, all.

PROPERTIUS   Caesar appeared in court.

MURENA   If we destroy our self-respect, allow
The dog authority to bark us quiet
Until custom prevents us peep out doors,
Self-prisoned in cramped jails of cowardice,
We are no longer Romans but tamed hares
Jugged when we least expect it, for a meal.
'God Caesar' triumphs. Are you a moral man?

PROPERTIUS   What must I do?

MURENA   Consult with Caepio;

I'll bring you to him. Hear what others say
Who voted for acquittal. Caesar plans
Wars against India.

PROPERTIUS   For pearl-heavy seas
And golden trophies . . .

MURENA   What's the difference?
Why should our Primus walk to execution
Like some barbarian king beneath defeat
For the same action?

PROPERTIUS   Plausible Murena,
I lost my home and father in the wars
On soil that now is peaceful under Rome.
You are Terentia's brother, Caesar's friend;
Maecenas' brother-in-law; his master trusts
Your loyalty.

MURENA   Would you put family
Before what's right, and let good Primus die?
Why, let morality chain up all claims,
If ties of blood condone dictatorship.

PROPERTIUS   You leave my words floating like leaves in air,
And do not listen. There's the Forum for
Debate, the Senate, too. We are all free.
Let me go to my world of poetry.
Fannius Caepio's not company
For men like you to keep.

MURENA   I know your mind—
Rebellious, yet as limp as apple-rind.
Think, quietly, what I've said, and when Fate
          smiles
Count us your friends among the crocodiles.

Exeunt.

SCENE FIFTEEN

MAECENAS *and* TERENTIA.

MAECENAS   Terentia, my wife.

TERENTIA   My husband?

MAECENAS   Come.

TERENTIA   Shall I sit by you?

MAECENAS   On my knee.

TERENTIA   For fun?

MAECENAS   If you love me.

TERENTIA   I do!

MAECENAS   My sparrow!

TERENTIA   Here!
          Have you some time for me today?

MAECENAS   I'm sorry.
          You know I act as Caesar's deputy
          Not least now he is suffering.

TERENTIA   Can I help?

MAECENAS   Have I denied you anything you asked?
          You share my palace on the Esquiline,
          Its birdsong gardens with their water wheels;
          And, though you've yet to see it, our estate
          In Egypt waits with flowering delta palms.
          Whatever gems, clothes, food or artistries
          Your heart has leapt for have—each time—been
                    yours.

TERENTIA   I love you for it! Fifteen is not old,
So you must teach me. I will learn from you
Culture and taste, whatever I should do
Or say on each occasion. All you ask
I'll do in gratitude unquestioning—
For my ambition throughout all my life
Is to be thought by you the perfect wife.

MAECENAS   My love. Then listen. Caesar is not well.
Remember who he is, what power he breathes.
He holds the world, responsibilities
So heavy most men would be crushed to paste
By just one pebble. Peace is his; and war—
Millions of lives. Terentia: he wants you.
Your youth and beauty like a moth at dusk
Lit in the flame of some high banquet torch
Stills conversation and makes all eyes soft.
Will you go to him, bathed, and in your pearls,
And pleasure him whatever silk unfurls?
Then you would pleasure me, keep our loved
        world
From danger, earn his blessing, and obey
Our trust with closed-eyed, quiet delicacy.
Come, say no more, my beauty. Not a word
Before, or after. I love you, my bird.

Fade.

SCENE SIXTEEN

CAESAR *and* VIRGIL.

CAESAR   Virgil, I am the only man in Rome
Who may not quarrel with his friend, and later
Forget the quarrel and be reconciled.
A ruler's anger is fatal. I've sad news.
My first Viceroy of Egypt, your school friend
And fellow-poet, Gallus—yes, Cornelius—
Has taken his own life while in disgrace.

VIRGIL   The seven-stringed lyre of Orpheus guide your
                        steps,
                  Gallus, so hoarfrost soothes and will not burn,
                  Nor rough ice pierce the softness of your foot;
                  And may that better land and broader sky
                  Where those who have enhanced mortality
                  With songs Apollo loves, be yours today.

CAESAR   I've tears for Gallus. It all went too far:
                  My anger, and his new-found arrogance
                  Once he reached Egypt. A revolt suppressed
                  In fifteen days at Thebaïd is carved,
                  With similar trivia, in three languages,
                  On the great pyramid. Statues the size
                  Of Rameses the Second, not of me
                  But him, scatter the country. Ask Valerius!
                  He whom I raised from nothing preened as
                        king,
                  Till Egypt's poison swelled, like Antony's.
                  He had to be disgraced: need not have died.

VIRGIL   His poems sang of a Propertius-like,
                  Tormented love for cruel Lycoris,
                  Once mistress of Brutus and Antony.
                  His elegiac couplets taught us that
                  Love conquers all. May your cool woods and
                        springs
                  Darkened, echo your songs up to the height
                  Where Vesper's evening star warns sheep to fold
                  As it sets out across the listening sky,
                  All heaven unwilling Gallus' song should die.

CAESAR   There's a sharp contrast with prosaic Agrippa,
                  With me at Apollonia as a boy,
                  Whose battles do deserve to be inscribed,
                  Though he will always step back from the glory.
                  I had to force the crown of Naulochus
                  On him. He's loyal: asks, consults, defers,
                  And spills his war-gold to enhance this city,
                  Not bullfrog out his self-aggrandizement.

VIRGIL   Caesar; not all your honoured ones are loyal.

CAESAR   What is implied?

VIRGIL   I hesitate to say,
                      And yet I am uneasy for you.

CAESAR   By
                      Our boyhood friendship, tell me.

VIRGIL   Yes, I will.
                      Do you remember how the Trojans gave
                      Pity to Sinon, as he swore to them
                      By Zeus and the eternal fires of heaven,
                      By altars, and by any loyalties
                      That yet remain unspoiled by men, that he,
                      Now welcomed by them from his desolation,
                      Would show his thanks; and brought the Trojan
                              horse?

CAESAR   I do.

VIRGIL   Our Sinon is Murena. He
                      Is plucking samples from mild discontent
                      To brew a poisoned chalice in your home.
                      It's always the loved Brutus holds the knife.

CAESAR   Man's terrifying misunderstanding of
                      All that he is appals me every day.
                      The sharpened awareness of the adulterer,
                      The heightened perception of the criminal
                      At point of crime, must be our safeguard now.
                      We lose our loved ones, when their minds grow
                              sick,
                      Like frantic blackbirds calling for their chick.
                      Leave this with me; and thank you.

                      Exit VIRGIL.

SCENE SEVENTEEN

Enter TERENTIA.

TERENTIA   May I come in?

CAESAR   Terentia! Of course.
               You have only to exist, even in absence,
               To charm, and bring release from thoughts of
                    force.

TERENTIA   Maecenas says you're ill?

CAESAR   My negligence
               Of health. These days I seem so mind-fatigued
               I do everything twice, I am so tense.

TERENTIA   Better than three times! Would you be intrigued
               If I stayed with you in my innocence?
               What pleases you? Would you like me to dance?

CAESAR   Youth, like the milk-white sea-spray, fades too
                    soon.
               What is a child but our own second chance
               Strangely provided by the punctual moon.

TERENTIA   Don't you want me?

CAESAR   Your loveliness could burn
               Pebbles to pearls. Maecenas must return.

               Fade.

SCENE EIGHTEEN

TERENTIA, *crying, to* MAECENAS.

MAECENAS   Terentia, my bride; how did it feel

With greatest Caesar? His cool breeze of
    autumn
Touched by first hints of frost?

TERENTIA   I'm so confused I don't know what to do,
What's right, or wicked; how I should behave.
You told me to go in and share his bed,
But his mind was on other things instead,
And anyway, he's courteous, and married,
And good to me. I feel ugly, and wrong.

MAECENAS   What did he say?

TERENTIA   You must go; help him cope.
I'll bath again and scrub my thoughts with soap.

Exit TERENTIA.

SCENE NINETEEN

CAESAR *and* MAECENAS.

CAESAR   Maecenas, you, my good friend, are in charge
Of our secret police.

MAECENAS   Octavian,
Joy was discreet. I am your bodyguard
For all emotions that are tense and strong.

CAESAR   What joy? The marriage! Yes, Agrippa's left
For Lesbos on a discreet mission to
Phraates of Parthia to return his son,
Held hostage by us, if he will return
Defeated Roman standards captured from
Crassus and Antony, with prisoners-of-war.
Those conquered eagles at Carrhae are still
A touchy subject; but Rome's gossips say
Over the laundry tub, through broken teeth,
Jealousy's driven Agrippa to the East

Jealous that our Marcellus now is heir.

MAECENAS   People will always swallow jealousy.
             They recognize it, and forget to probe.

CAESAR   I've something difficult for you to do.

MAECENAS   What else?

CAESAR   Your feelings will be hurt, as mine
             Have been: but a conspiracy's alleged.
             Will you find out—discreetly, carefully—
             Murena's plans? I want to question him.

MAECENAS   Murena! He's all sarcasm and air!
             Look in the Law Courts; you will find him there.

CAESAR   I shall. You know my doctor, Antony Musa,
             Who cured me once with chilled drinks and
                     cold baths?
             He's treating our Marcellus.

MAECENAS   He is ill?

CAESAR   A fever shakes his body. He can't see.

MAECENAS   Musa will cure him.

CAESAR   I'll be with Marcellus.

             Exeunt.

                    SCENE TWENTY

             HORACE *and* MURENA.

HORACE   Murena, you've been Consul with Octavian—
             'Augustus' as the Senate calls him, now
             He has transferred the Republic from his power

Back to the Senate and People of Rome . . .

MURENA
He still
Is Consul for ten years! His provinces—
Spain, Gaul and Syria, Cyprus, Egypt—have
Some twenty legions sworn to him alone.
The name, but not the power, has changed.

HORACE
My friend.
When sailing, it's best not to hug the coast
With all its dangers, nor press out to sea.
Those who value the Golden Mean in life—
Not a slum home, nor palace—live secure
From envy. It's the tall pine shakes in gales.
When things go wrong, hope; have faith. When
    success
Warms your wide sky, be aware all can change.

MURENA
Poems are rafts of language on the sea
Of time, puffed by the gusts of life.
You can accept the natural world, but I
Spurn acquiescence in its process, claim
The searching, limitless reaches of man's mind.
What is our cry for infinite power but this?

Enter TERENTIA.

HORACE
Your sister's here.

MURENA
Why tears, Terentia?

TERENTIA
My husband whispered to me that a warrant
For your arrest is issued.

MURENA
I must leave.
Horace, I'll let out sail in these storm winds.

HORACE
The gods give us bleak winters but warm
    springs.

Exeunt.

Procession to the Mausoleum.

MESSALLA   Make way, and hear! I speak to you as Augur.
            We bring Rome's first gift to the mausoleum,
            A youth of beauty and of brilliance;
            And if the whispers of the circling crowd
            Ask who it is, answer, a noble presence,
            High-born, expectant; shadowed by nightfall.
            Fate lent him to us for the briefest stay
            Afraid that Rome might grow too strong to pray.
            Brave men of Mars, show now in Mars's city
            What mourning lamentation we can give.
            Old-fashioned honour's buried, dead in him.
            Grant me to strew, by handfuls, purple lilies
            And with such gifts at least endow his shade
            With ineffectual duty. Emulate him,
            And you shall be Marcellus. On! Make way!

            Exeunt.

CAESAR *and* AGRIPPA.

CAESAR   Marcellus rests inside my mausoleum—
            Built to show Rome though Antony might lie
            Beside a Ptolemaic queen, with kings
            In shifting sands of Egypt, Caesar's shade
            Rules from a great park built for all citizens
            Here at the centre of the world; their own.
            There that young body, scattered with our
                    flowers,
            Remains for all time, child of our lost hopes.
            Virgil's great words, spoken by Messalla,
            Ring in our ears. The grieving mother, Octavia,

When we heard Virgil read them yesterday,
Fell down unconscious when she heard him sigh:
'Boy, worth our pity! Heu! miserande puer . . .'
You have returned from Phraates just in time
To mourn Marcellus. Tell me what happened.

AGRIPPA
                                                Now?
When you are torn with grief? Well, it may help.
I mentioned several legions were at hand;
And that his son was with me.

CAESAR
                                   Did he see
The argument?

AGRIPPA
                       It was persuasive.

CAESAR
                     And?

AGRIPPA
I have the captured standards; all the Romans
Taken as prisoners-of-war except
Those who've died, or gone native.

CAESAR
                             I'll decree
My temple, vowed at Philippi to avenge
My father's murder, be completed to
Receive the returning eagles, won by us
With peace which had been lost before in
      battle;
And Julius Caesar's half-built theatre
Shall be named Theatre of Marcellus. Superb
Agrippa. You must marry Julia,
My widowed, young teen daughter. You are still
Younger than Maecenas. I know your wife
Marcella, my sister's daughter, is still alive,
But you have seldom seen her, being abroad:
And if you marry Julia, your son
Will be my heir. Julia's attractive, rounded . . .

AGRIPPA
Divorce Marcellus' sister at this time
For a third marriage, to your only child?
Caesar, my conscience of things left undone

For both my previous wives jerks me awake
Like midnight cramp at times. I'll start again.

CAESAR   My friend becomes my son; your sons, our fame.

Exit AGRIPPA.

SCENE TWENTY-THREE

CAESAR *and* MAECENAS.

MAECENAS   You've raised obscure Agrippa now so high—
Admiral, victorious general, diplomat,
War-minister, bringing the standards home
Of Crassus with no loss of Roman blood—
That you must either kill him, or embrace
Your equal as your son-in-law!

CAESAR   You listen
With an acute ear through the door. Maecenas,
During our wars with Sextus Pompey, you
I made Deputy Head of State. Although
You run the secret police, huge crowds gave you
A warm ovation in the theatre
After your illness. I've consulted you,
In delicate matters of diplomacy,
Almost lieutenant Emperor. Why then
Betray my trust when my whole life's at risk
To let Murena run? And, to a girl!

MAECENAS   My wife. Yours if . . .

CAESAR   From now your close advisership of me
Goes to Sallustius Crispus.

MAECENAS   Octavian!
It just slipped out!

CAESAR   If trust is broken when one's life's at stake

Don't be too startled if close friendships break.
Our intimacy formed in Apollonia
When news came to me of my destiny.
You steered, helped, guided me through
      desperate years
Till I am what you see. Out of my sight!
Send Virgil!

Exit MAECENAS.

SCENE TWENTY-FOUR

Enter VIRGIL.

CAESAR   Longest-lasting, loyalest friend.
My health deteriorates. Look! Here I wear
A seal-skin amulet to ward off lightning.
On a night march in Cantabria once
A flash of Jupiter the Thunderer grazed
My litter and struck dead the wide-eyed slave
Carrying a torch in front of me. Virgil,
Have you fresh news? Has Murena been caught?

VIRGIL   Neither Caepio nor Murena stood
Trial, so were convicted through default.
Murena was hit by a flying wheel
And axle, as he turned; knocked to the ground.
Turnus scythed his sword-blade across between
The helmet's lower edge and breastplate's top.
The severed head and trunk's left on the sand.

CAESAR   Sinon indeed! The ultimate betrayal
Is when the family itself, the miniature
Of our whole state, turns inward to destroy.

VIRGIL   Not only Rome but Judea suffers. Herod
Has killed the wife he so adored. Mariammë
Never forgave his murder of her father:
A bad start to their marriage. Lust on one side,

Fury responded. But two sons of theirs,
Alexander and Aristobulus,
Have just arrived in Rome; staying with Pollio—
A gentile, which has raised some Jewish
        eyebrows—
To try the lecture-rooms, and to forget.

CAESAR   If she tried poison on him, she deserves
Every just punishment. Pollio's house!
Why, they can come here! I will father them
And they'll be safe. All princes are at risk.
When Pollio was Consul, Antony
Married my sister as a guarantee
Of love and peace—that Cleopatra ruined.
You wrote a poem for your early patron
Drawing on Pollio's love of Jewish dreams.
I wish all had come true. O, Antony!

VIRGIL   You yourself have brought peace into the world,
And a new child, perhaps of Julia,
Will bring our age of Saturn back to earth,
Proving the Sybil's song of Cumae true.
Lucina, you who bless us to the light,
Goddess of childbirth, help virgin Astraea
Bring forth a son to rule a world in which
His father's virtues have brought peace.

CAESAR   Virgil,
Your vision, in its purity, sustains
A sick man tired of fear and treachery.
Stay with me while I sleep, and trim the light.
Your thoughts, weightless as wind, will calm my
        night.

Fade.

END OF ACT ONE

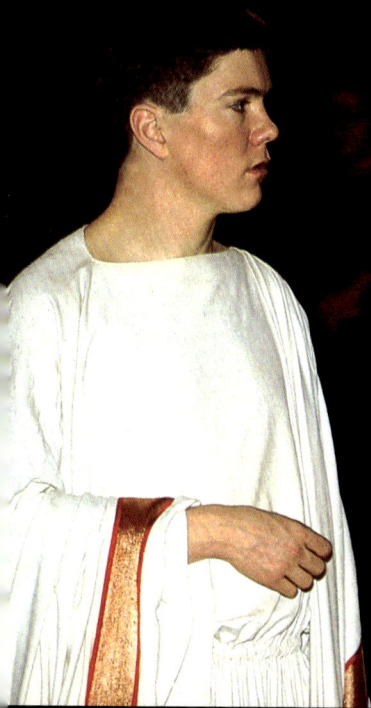

Act Two

MAECENAS*'s symposium;* HORACE, PROPERTIUS, VIRGIL.

MAECENAS   Welcome to celebration! Fill your bowls!
Each in turn shall be master of the grape.
I legislate: nine ladles wine, three water.
Here from the saucer's unmixed wine I offer
Libation. Apollo's statue is complete,
(His face? The Emperor's) and now unveiled
In the Palatine Temple Library.
Yes! All your immortality, my poets,
And all you've yet to bring to birth, lives there.

Applause.

Yes, yes; I paid a little towards it; some;
But Rome without a library is dumb!
And, on a more domestic note, today's
The anniversary of our jaunt together
Along that queen of roads, the Appian Way,
Horace, through your Apulian, sirocco hills,
Till we met Pollio at Brundisium.

HORACE   In a barge, towed, Maecenas, till you joined us.
Our boatman, once we were shut-eyed, turned
    out
His mule to graze, and snored loud on his back.
This woke some hot-head passenger, who
    jumped
Out on the tow-path; with a willow-club
Thumped both the mule and boat-man head
    and tail.
Virgil, you, Plotius and Varius,
Met us at Sinuessa; missed the frogs'
Croaking, wrecking our rocking, gnat-buzzed
    sleep.

MAECENAS   Oh, it was fun! We cheered two jokers' joust
            Not with fists but inane insults. One dusk
            You paid a girl, and waited till midnight,
            And were left standing! Then, at Beneventum,
            Near-burned to death when our painstaking
                    host,
            Roasting some skinny thrushes on his spit
            For us, made a volcano of the embers
            Which crumbling sent flames up into the roof.
            Ah, all the hungry guests and terrified slaves
            First grabbed their plates, then tried to fight the
                    blaze.

VIRGIL   You energetically played ball-games—
            Not good for those with sore eyes, or dyspeptics.
            Murena kindly lodged us at Formiae.

MAECENAS   Murena! What a sharp chill crawls down my
                    spine.
            Murena helped Octavian in those days.
            You've written, Virgil: 'Is it so terrible
            A thing to die?' Don't palliate death away.
            I'd rather limp behind a plough for lentils,
            A chained slave-peasant bullied by a brat,
            Than reign as king of all the buried dead.

PROPERTIUS You, who have held the highest office when
            Caesar has been away—some years back, now—
            You could be juggling justice in the Forum,
            Or win war's glory through the Parthian spears,
            Nailing their trophies to your palace walls!
            But you step modestly into the shadows;
            In conscious choice you furl your ship's full
                    sail—
            And you are wise! You, too, will be remembered,
            As our dead Gallus is, whose wounds of love
            From his cruel beauty, Lycoris, are soothed
            In the dark waters of the world below.

HORACE   (*Taking his turn in charge of the wine*)
            We've become morbid, and the wine's not drunk.

Come now! A health to the new moon, and
    praise
Murena's good side: skill in augury.

VIRGIL

He was adopted by erudite Varro,
And became half-brother to Proculeius—
One of the last to see Queen Cleopatra
Just before she died. Murena learned
His augury from Varro, as I learned
How to make Greek wine from him, and dip
    sheep:
A thoughtful teacher . . .

HORACE

                    And encyclopaedist.
I learned most from my father. He was poor,
As farmers go, yet sent me to school in Rome,
And came with me to all tutorials.
Next, from Maecenas most. It was not chance
Brought us together. Virgil—best of men—
And Varius had told you who I was.
I blushed in hesitation when we met,
And shyness made me stammer. I told you
My father was a freed slave. You said little.
I left. Time passed; and then, full nine months
    later,
You brought me back to be among your friends.

PROPERTIUS

I, too, adopt your rule of life, Maecenas.
You give me such reflected glory, I
May be included when men count your friends.

HORACE

You lead each girl to every jerking dance
Till passion flows out at her fingertips.
Next, she'll be leaving husband at dessert
(He knows) to meet some foreign sailor lad
Spending his shore pay on her furtive dark.
These weren't the parents who fought
    Hannibal.

MAECENAS

Have you been influenced by Augustus, Horace?
He seems obsessed with his new marriage laws,

Curbing licentiousness. This time they'll pass.
Adultery will be criminal: each lose
Much of their property, each of them banished
for
Life onto different islands . . .

VIRGIL   (*Taking his turn in charge of the wine*) Our love
poetry
Of elegiac couplets is uncoupled.
Rome will regret this—weep for elegy!

PROPERTIUS   Widows have twelve months to remarry in;
Divorcees six.

VIRGIL   What use are laws and courts
To a passionate woman? Great sorrow wrecks
the heart,
And grief streams bitterness from sweetest lips.

MAECENAS   Yet Caesar tolerates Timagenes
Who, old and popular, attacks Augustus,
Publicly burns all tributes in the street.
Augustus has of course banned him the palace,
But nothing more. Pollio gives him lodging.
All that Augustus said when Pollio dined
Was 'Do you keep a zoo?' 'If you tell me to,
I'll kick him out at once.' 'Would I do that?'
Said Caesar. 'I've reconciled you two again.
Make the most of him!'

VIRGIL   Julius Caesar, too,
Could tolerate. Once, when the young Catullus
Read out rude verse on Caesar's engineer,
Mamurra, and against Julius himself
(Caesar was dining with Catullus' father),
The boy was scolded. When he apologized,
Julius Caesar invited him to dinner!
I was thirteen, fishing in the Mincius,
When tanned Catullus in his yacht came by
Towed by two mules past our home. He
stopped,

And father gave him vegetables; I
A parody of his verse-panegyric
Celebrating his yacht. Mine sang the mules.

HORACE

He's lucky. Julius could be intolerant.
At Uxellodunum all who'd opposed him had
Their hands cut off on his strict orders. I
Sleep, on the whole, till ten a.m.; then read,
Or write something; rub myself down with oil;
Go for a stroll, alone, wherever whim takes me;
Ask the price of flour, and vegetables;
Circle the Circus Maximus, avoiding
Tricksters with stalls in the outer walls; walk
    down
The Forum, overhear the fortune-tellers,
Then home to a dish of pancakes, leeks and
    peas.
This way I hope I'll live more pleasantly
Than if my many ancestors had been
Quartermasters, junior bankers, librarians.

PROPERTIUS

(*Taking his turn in charge of the wine*)
Maecenas, when the Fates require my life,
And I become a name on a small piece
Of marble, should your travels bring you near
(You hope and envy of the young!) please halt
Your yoked and hand-carved British chariot
And, with a tear, on my long-silent ashes,
Murmur 'A cruel girl wrecked this sad man.'

MAECENAS

I shall, Propertius. Be that time far off!
Before then, all of us shall have another
Party, like this: I will read with you
Each taking turns—my own Symposium
I've written, in which Virgil, Horace, Messalla
(Alas! Reading the guts of birds today
On Temple duty), each has a part to speak.

PROPERTIUS

I'll read Messalla's, if he's auguring,
But please! no parody of me. Too easy!
Just think of me as Rome's Callimachus.

HORACE   Callimachus! Starved Greek love-elegist?
                I'll scratch your back if you'll scratch mine. By
                     this
                I am Alcaeus! You Callimachus?
                More like . . . minor Mimnérmus of Colophon,
                Primitive, early; yes: Mimnérmus, you.
                O, nothing is better than cheerful companions
                As we all were, Maecenas, when you met
                Antony at Brundisium, and brought
                Us with you for the ride. O for the days
                That are lost to me, lost to me . . .

PROPERTIUS   Virgil, some water. You love your Mincius,
                Reed-fringed, meandering lazily, and I
                The branches where light spills through leaves
                     to wash
                White oxen cooling in Clitumnus' stream.
                Ah, Gallus, you'd have praised it till all Muses
                Crowned your sad gentleness our Hesiod.

VIRGIL   Gallus drifts by the streams of Helicon
                Where a god's son, a shepherd-poet of
                Immortal song, hatted with scattered flowers
                And bitter parsley, gives him the Muses' reed-
                     pipe—
                Hesiod's once—urging him honour in echoing
                Music Apollo's consecrated trees.
                Agrippa comes. We must away, look forward;
                Not back to tragedy and Actium.
                Come warriors of verse! Hold out your cups
                In your right hands! I'll wreathe his hair with
                     leaves—
                A crown in honour of this feast, Maecenas!

                Exeunt MAECENAS *and* VIRGIL.

                          SCENE TWO

HORACE   Propertius, just a word before we leave.

You're getting bumptious and, yes, I can tell
    you,
Making a fool of yourself these days. I mean it!
If a grown man ties mice to a small box
On wheels, or rides a hobbyhorse, or builds
Tree houses, people say he is insane.
If reason proves that being in love is childish,
Then mucking about in the dust or, sillier still,
Whining and moping for a prostitute
Is equally infantile: 'Shall I go to her?
Will she let me in? She's banged the door.
Shall I forget it all? She's opened—beckons!
Shall I go back to her? Never! Not if she begs
    me . . .'
Love has two evils: war, and peace—both fickle
As the weather. Your bitch you follow like a pup,
Wagging for Cynthia. Take my advice: grow up.

Exit PROPERTIUS.

SCENE THREE

Enter AGRIPPA.

AGRIPPA   Horace! What are you doing, flushed with wine
Like this?

HORACE   Maecenas' party.

AGRIPPA   Ah! The poets.
Have you written my ode yet?

HORACE   Agrippa,
You should be praised in verse by Varius,
A poet of Homeric power, and brave
Enough to write of your huge ships and wars.
I am too feeble for the mighty themes.
The peaceful Muse warns me to know my place,
Not trivialize the Emperor, or yourself.

I sing of banquets, girls' sharp fingernails
Warring with adolescents; songs of love;
Whether I happen to be hooked or not.

AGRIPPA

My hobby, as I rattle round the world,
Is working out the coastlines, bays, where I
Can shelter, spring an ambush, from a hill
Look into enemy country. I'm compiling,
For our Augustus and my peace of mind,
A map of the world, and need your learned
        help.
Leave out the Muses' Garden—all that fiction.
I'm not impervious to the arts. Far from it.
My map will be displayed for all to use
In my new park, east of the Via Lata.
What I should like's a law to nationalize
All valuable art in private hands,
So that the citizens could come to see
Treasures of human spirit in the temples.

HORACE

A good Republican! But might the nobles
Notice their privacy invaded? Art
Would lose its value with no market-place.

AGRIPPA

I've built a temple to all gods. It's best
Not to leave Juno out; or Venus, Mars,
Julius Caesar. The lot. The Pantheon.
Come and walk round it with me.

HORACE

                                You who are
Married to the Emperor's daughter, given a tent
Exactly like his when on joint campaigns—
All military orders signed by both—
Agrippa, you are half the ruling power.

AGRIPPA

The junior half—and anyway, I'm not.
I am his empire-builder, reflected in
Rome's marble rising all around; temples,
Arches and porticoes, baths, monuments.
Are your works safely in our Library?

HORACE   My monument's more permanent than bronze,
          Loftier than the royal pyramids;
          One that no rain, or tempests, can destroy,
          Or years consume into oblivion.
          Not all of me shall die: my better part
          Lives in your Library.

AGRIPPA   Good, that's a start.

                         SCENE FOUR

          Enter CAESAR *and* MESSALLA.

CAESAR   Agrippa, hail! Horace, I'm pleased to catch you.
          Do you have any influence with Virgil?
          I wrote, begging him, even threatening,
          (In fun) for at least the outline of his poem,
          His epic on me, his *Aeneid*—or just
          A single section of his choice.

MESSALLA   Replied?

CAESAR   He writes to me: 'Such an enormous task
          Is started, that I think I must have been
          Touched by the moon to have undertaken it.'

HORACE   Lunatic? Virgil? No! Whitest of men,
          Whose style is deft and tender.

CAESAR   Will you see
          What you can do on my behalf?

HORACE   I will,
          Augustus.

CAESAR   I shall need a poem from you,
          Short, but effective, on my Marriage Laws.
          It's a new world, my Horace.

HORACE   A world where
The chastity of parents is their gift
To each, and to their children. Husbands shrink
From wives of other men. The price of sin
Is death.

CAESAR   Exactly. Soon we shall celebrate
Five centuries of Roman power. A hymn
Is needed. It will be performed high on
The Palatine hill, in front of the Library-temple.
I shall be standing by Apollo's statue
Which holds the poets' musical instrument;
But at his feet the bow of vengeance lies.

HORACE   (*Startled*) Yes! Yes!

CAESAR   Men sing some verses, women
          other:
Twenty-six voices each, as is our custom.
How you do it is up to you.

HORACE   I see.
But make the point about licentiousness
Extirpated, and anti-social spinsters
And bachelors?

CAESAR   What I like in verse
Are precepts, aphorisms, I can note
And send to members of my family—
Julia; or to Senators; governors
Of provinces, to generals at war.
Rules to live by. Can you do this for me?

HORACE   Leaders impose the laws of marriage, destined
To breed prolific, healthy, happy offspring,
And see our harvests blest with fertile rain.

CAESAR   Yes, that's the sort of thing. Don't forget peace!
You will be paid.

          Exit HORACE.

SCENE FIVE

CAESAR   The nicest little man,
The purest prick I know.

MESSALLA   Maecenas made him.

CAESAR   I want my name to live. That means the poets
Must give their best. I'm writing my own life;
And our great mausoleum dominates
The Tiber's bank as your fine Pantheon,
Agrippa, balances it in your park,
Its vaulted roof rocking the sky's own dome:
Two marble breasts of Rome that feed the eyes,
The imaginations, of all citizens
And foreigners: twin fountains of Rome's peace.

AGRIPPA   Caesar, your genius lives among the months
To furthest time. Your spear-held statue stands
Inside my Pantheon. May I name both
After Augustus?

CAESAR   No, Agrippa. Never
Dedicate the temple of all gods
To me. That would be hubris.

AGRIPPA   We need your luck.
The river's overflowed, is spreading plague,
And everyone cries out: 'Make you Dictator!'

MESSALLA   The mob locked in the Senators and yelled
They'd torch the building roof and sides, unless
They voted you full dictatorial powers.
Twenty-four men with Lictors' rods now beg
You take command over the corn supply,
As Pompey did.

CAESAR   Well; if I must, I will:

But never try to make me a Dictator.
I want to be a private citizen,
Write my biography, and see my child.

AGRIPPA   Small hope at present. All depends on you.
Beyond the city, your great provinces
Thirst for your visit to them. Mightiest power
Falters when turned away; dies in neglect.

MESSALLA   After discussion, at the moment of
Consensus, vote; or it evaporates.
The self-importance of the hurrying
Senators is their Achilles' heel.
You can appropriate this moment well
By taking charge, then travelling abroad.
A comet's tail streams away from the sun.

CAESAR   Never Dictator. No. Limited power
For a fixed period. Come out of this shower.

Exeunt AGRIPPA *and* MESSALLA.

SCENE SIX

Enter JULIA.

CAESAR   My Julia, inevitably I
See less of you than I should. When Murena
Tried with his rabble to kill me, I sent
You to the safety of an island. There
An old and feeble forger, Audasius,
With a Parthian half-breed, Epicadus,
Planned through their haggard minds to kidnap
                you
And your small baby by Agrippa—Gaius—
To take you to the legions. Your protection
Had to take precedence over fatherly contact.
Always these endless cares of state! I have
Neglected to teach you about such things
As augury, and Virgil's bees—their habits.

JULIA   I'm all ears, Father.

CAESAR   That's the problem; yes!

JULIA   I think I know what you mean.

CAESAR   Procreation!
                You seem to think of very little else.

JULIA   Rather a fancy term for sex?

CAESAR   Not so.
                Regeneration, creativity,
                Are the two golden gifts of God. They find
                Supreme perfection in a baby boy.

JULIA   I agree; but the regenerative urge,
                Father—you know—is imprisoned in the senses:
                Therefore the senses should be stroked and
                    trained,
                As by a fine athlete, to keep in trim
                And be creative in regeneration.

CAESAR   Now; back to bees. They do not copulate,
                Or stale their energies when Venus drives,
                Or in rough groans push offspring to the world,
                But delicately find their children in
                Mouths of sweet smelling herbs, as Virgil writes.
                His father was a stone-blind bee-keeper,
                Who taught him all. He knows.

JULIA   I'm not a bee.
                I am your daughter: female.

CAESAR   There you're right!
                Females slowly burn up, waste men's strength.
                Bulls, for a simpering heifer, clash their horns
                In violent butting: black blood floods their sides
                As they tear open wounds in bellowing.
                You can't control a horse who scents a mare
                On heat; and mares, short of a stallion,

In spring go mad. They stand in line together
On some high cliff, and let the spring wind fill
    them,
Miraculously pregnant by hot air.

JULIA   I'm not a heifer, nor a mare.

CAESAR   Exactly!
You know, it is not easy for a father
To explain to a daughter finer points
Of growing up, especially when she
Has four times been engaged, twice married,
    and
Has a small son. Julia, what I'm saying
Is, I am trying, desperately, to create
A finer Rome, in which unfaithfulness
And libertine behaviour are curtailed.
How can I do this if my family
Itself sets no example? You're nineteen.
Try not to talk, or think, of things obscene.

JULIA   Didn't you in your early twenties give
A fancy-dress banquet for the Divine Twelve—
Six goddesses, six gods? Gods wear no clothes.
Antony named all the guests in that frolic.

CAESAR   And look what lust has done to Antony!
Julia; be the daughter all expect
Of a priest-leader of a world empire.
Avoid impure thoughts. Study augury.
Find a good hobby: birds' eggs. Read Lucretius.

JULIA   Father, I'm sorry if malicious gossip
Has caused embarrassment. I'll try to stop it.

Exit CAESAR.

SCENE SEVEN

Enter PROPERTIUS.

JULIA   My father is impossible! Oh, Propertius
              I am glad you are here.

PROPERTIUS   Why? What's upset you?

JULIA   Gossip has reached him. He is not specific:
              Doubtless all of it's true. Father's forgotten
              What it's like to be teenaged, young, and
                    healthy,
              Spreeing along life's coast, coasting life's spree.

PROPERTIUS   Children never forgive their parents for
              Not being what they were.

JULIA   Oh, I reminded
              Him of the banquet he gave for the naked
                    twelve
              Immortals, and how Antony told Rome.

PROPERTIUS   His sense of humour tickled?

JULIA   Sex and I
              For him don't mix.

PROPERTIUS   You are a mother!

JULIA   Ah;
              I thought I understood my body, but
              It's just too difficult.

PROPERTIUS   Sprawling briar-rose
              That forced back, plucked, grows lovelier?

JULIA   You know women!

PROPERTIUS   I can unite quarrelling lovers apart,
                   Ease open a mistress' reluctant doors;
                   Can cure another lover's newest wounds.
                   The power of my healing words is strong.

JULIA   Bring lovers together? Iulus Antony,
                   Come back! Come back!

PROPERTIUS   Iulus Antony!
                   Mark Antony's son by Fulvia? Surely not
                   A sweaty bed with Caesar's clemency,
                   The spared son of your father's enemy?

JULIA   You're just as bad with married Cynthia.
                   Why don't you leave her? There are other girls
                   Who'll close their eyes with chins up just for you.

PROPERTIUS   I've tried. She has so flagrantly abused
                   Our bed, so often, I thought I'd dig my trench
                   Elsewhere; move camp. Phyllis I know lives near
                   Diana's temple on the Aventine.
                   Sober, she's less than attractive; tipsy, charming.
                   And there's another—Teia, near Tarpeia
                   Woods, looks fresh as daybreak, but when drunk
                   One man alone is not enough to slake
                   Her. I asked them round to comfort my night,
                   Cheer up my drooping self with something new.
                   In a secluded garden we'd a couch
                   For three. I was between them. Lygdamus
                   Served us Greek vintage wine in summer
                        tumblers,
                   A Nile-boy played the flutes; our rose-scattered
                        girl,
                   Artlessly elegant, the castanets.
                   We had the dwarf, clapping his stunted hands
                   To the box-wood flutes. The omens were not
                        good:
                   Full lamps died down; the table fell; my dice
                   Never threw luck. The girls sang: I was deaf.
                   Undid their breasts for me: but I was blind,
                   My mind was elsewhere. Suddenly the gates

Rasped open. A commotion filled the hall.
Cynthia slammed wide each of the garden doors,
Her hair infuriatingly attractive. Glass
Slipped from my fingers, and my wine-red lips
Turned white. Her eyes lightninged with flame.
    She raged
As only a woman can, and shoved her nails
In Phyllis's face, while Teia yelled out 'Fire!'
The street woke up. The ripped and stripped
    girls ran
To the nearest tavern. Cynthia held high her
    spoils,
Hurried back, punched my face and bit my neck
Till the blood ran; aimed for my guilty eyes.
When her arms tired, she spotted Lygdamus
Hiding behind the couch and dragged him out.
I begged her terms. Disdainfully, exulting,
She sneered: 'Don't swagger Pompey's colonnade;
Nor hang about the Forum for the fights;
Nor peer round flirting at the theatre;
Nor peep when a litter exposes itself to you;
Above all, sell this slave—chained from each
    foot.'

JULIA   No!

PROPERTIUS   Lygdamus, I had no more power than you!

JULIA   You coward!

PROPERTIUS   I said: 'I accept!' She gloated;
Disinfected where those girls had sat,
And touched. Washed down the threshold.
    Made me empty
All the oil lamps; and next—re-fuel them.
Three times she fumed my head with sulphur.
    Then,
When every sheet and blanket had been
    changed,
I kissed her. We made peace throughout our bed.

Exit PROPERTIUS.

Enter TERENTIA.

JULIA   I can't wait for our party. I've arranged
               The Forum will be closed at dusk, so we
               Shall have it to ourselves for a wild dance
               Till sunrise. Even the Rostra will be ours.
               Did you find good books in the library?

TERENTIA   Yes. Yours is on contraception. Mine, I hope,
               Will make me fertile.

JULIA   Read me some. Yours first.

TERENTIA   'The soul creates the mould of your new foetus.
               Girls who watch monkeys during intercourse
               Produce monkey-like children. Breeders turn
               Mares to face noble horses during covering.'

JULIA   And we should leer at athletes?

TERENTIA   We must be sober,
               Or our drunk fantasies will stamp the child.

JULIA   I don't believe it! Useful tips for me?

TERENTIA   For contraception good Hippocrates
               Recommends leaping with the heels to
                   buttocks.
               It aids expulsion.

JULIA   (*Leaps*) I'm exhausted!

TERENTIA   Goat's bladder
               For a man; re-use. For us? Liver of a cat:
               Place in a tube and tie to the left foot.
               Open a hairy spider's head, and take
               The two small, wriggling worms out; bind them in

A deerskin; wear it during lovemaking.

JULIA   Anything less sartorial?

TERENTIA   Pinebark, tanning
                 Sumach, equal quantities of each,
                 Rub well with wine, wrap wool around, apply;
                 After three hours, remove it: then make love.
                 Or: grind fresh pomegranate peel, and apply.
                 Or: grind two parts of pomegranate peel to
                 One part of oak galls. Or: unripe oak galls,
                 With inside pomegranate peel, ginger (two
                      drachms),
                 Mould it with wine to the size of vetch peas
                 And dry indoors, then, carefully, make love.
                 Or: grind the flesh of dried figs, apply with
                      natron.
                 Or: pomegranate peel, with oil of roses, and
                      gum.

JULIA   Gum?

TERENTIA   Gum. Glue. Make it stick. This should be
                      followed
                 With a cold drink of honey water. Last:
                 At the critical moment hold your breath.

JULIA   My father ordered me to read Lucretius,
                 Who says 'Wriggle the ploughshare from the
                      furrow.'
                 That sounds more like good farming sense to me.
                 Tonight we'll chaos with the golden boys,
                 The sons of consuls, all our wealth enjoys,
                 Fun and lighthearted summer recklessness,
                 Drinks laced with irresponsibility;
                 Chatter and laughter, truanting all cares,
                 Gaiety, charm, wit, our high youth is theirs.
                 I'm flushed with expectation! Help me dress;
                 Then I'll parade there in my loveliness.

                 Exeunt.

Enter AGRIPPA *and* CAESAR.

AGRIPPA   Caesar, Herod is here; asks your permission
            To kill his sons.

CAESAR   His sons ? My friends! But why?
            I've said all princes are at risk, but not
            From their own fathers!

AGRIPPA   Well, that's what he wants.

CAESAR   I'd rather be Herod's pig than Herod's son.

AGRIPPA   At least he'd not touch pork. Will you try them
            In open court?

CAESAR   Brief me.

AGRIPPA   When the two boys,
            Alexander and Aristobulus,
            Mariammë's sons by Herod, went from Rome,
            Gilt with the tincture of your patronage,
            To hot Judaea, Herod's sister, Salome,
            Spread rumours that they planned to murder
                Herod.
            She had destroyed their mother; now she fears
            The vengeance of the sons.

CAESAR   Herod believes this?

AGRIPPA   He is emotional. His sister hates
            The Hasmonaeans. After Mariammë
            Had walked with dignity to execution,
            Plague swarmed his country; even honoured
                friends
            Of Herod, pampered, aloof, spilled into graves.
            Herod called back an elder son of his

By a non-Hasmonaean girl, and he—
Called Antipas—connived then with Salome
To lead the two boys on to mourn their mother,
And use this evidence of grief as proof
Of treason.

CAESAR   I see.

AGRIPPA   Herod treated me well—
Generously—when I hunted Scribonius
Out on the Bosphorus. He's turned Strato's
        Tower,
You gave him, into a seething trading city;
Dug a new harbour for it, Portus Augusti,
And named it Caesarea.

CAESAR   For the Jews?

AGRIPPA   No. For the Greeks and Syrians, but Jews
Flock in.

CAESAR   There will be trouble there one day.
At the Red Sea I needed reinforcements
For Aelius Gallus' troops. Herod helped with
Five hundred of his own picked bodyguards.
Well; I'll tread carefully among the coals;
It is the deadly snake music controls.
Please fetch them.

Exit AGRIPPA.

SCENE TEN

Enter VIRGIL.

CAESAR   Virgil, gentle sanity!
I gave my Julia some advice, and cash:
Two hundred and fifty denarii—the sum
I throw each of my dinner guests for gambling—

To modesty a daughter's waywardness,
And Herod asks my leave to strangle his sons!
A ruler's family is the calm centre
Around which turns an unrelenting world.
Destroy that peace, and Armageddon comes.
Is his miraculous success in public
Worth the grim cost in tragedies at home?

VIRGIL Blest is that man whose understanding sees
Through to the causes of all things, and treads
Under his feet inexorable Fate
And all irrational fears and jealousies—
A man like our Lucretius . . .

CAESAR   Killed himself
At forty-four, having been poisoned mad
By a love-philtre.

VIRGIL   Yet Lucretius knew
The harmony that heals this natural world,
And the strange pathos of our earthly life.

CAESAR 'Extending days does not contract to shorten
Our everlasting darkness'—so he writes.
'All love is mixed with pain; it never finds
More than thin images to satisfy.'
Though marvellous poetry, it will not do
As a philosophy. The Julian comet
Has blazed across our sky to herald peace,
A dawn of fervent longing freed from war—
Saturn's new age at last, the years of gold
When doors of Janus' temple shall be closed.
Despair, and weariness of heart are healed.
Our altar of Fortune Returning at the gate
Through which we brought the Crassus
          standards home
To holiday Rome is carved with patterned vines
Of Paradise.

VIRGIL   (*Holding coins*) Julia's denarii
Stamped with submission of the Parthians

Show Crassus' standards and recaptured eagles
In your new temple of Mars the Avenger.
Another pictures, standing on a globe,
Winged Victory with wreath; and, yes, one glows
Your divine father Julius with his comet.

CAESAR   Augustan peace imaged in gold and silver
Scatters the world like hope at winter's death.

VIRGIL   Is there no limit beyond which the curse
Of greed for gold compels men's hearts?

CAESAR   We ride it,
Deflecting greed to admiration!
May I hear how your poem honours us
Now the Republic is restored to Rome,
Peace suckles wealth throughout our provinces,
And finer morals are enshrined in law?
Is the *Augusteid* ready that you promised
In your third *Georgic*, back in the heady days
Of Actium?

VIRGIL   Not, Caesar, as I hoped,
A poem celebrating works and days
Of our Augustus, glancing backward to
Rome's ancestors from Troy. No. That reversed:
Aeneas' odyssey from burning Troy
To our lush Italy, with glimpses of
A destined future for almighty Rome
Revealed to Aeneas by his father's shade—
Unconquerable empire, rich, and free,
Imposing world peace, ruled at last by you.
'Augustus Caesar, son of deity,
Who will restore the golden centuries
Of Saturn farther than the Indians
And Garamant, a world beyond the stars . . .'

CAESAR   Acceptable. King Herod and his sons
Wait for me. I must welcome them, and comfort
Their travel-weariness with friendly care
And freshest treasures from our countryside.

When parents and their children are at odds
We shame the beasts; we, who might well be gods.

Exit VIRGIL.

SCENE ELEVEN

Enter AGRIPPA, MESSALLA, HEROD, ARISTOBULUS,
ALEXANDER.

CAESAR   Herod, welcome! Agrippa tells me you
Feasted him in Judaea with luxury,
Showed him the harbour you named after me,
The fortresses of Alexandreion,
Herodion, your rebuilt Hyrcania;
That in Jerusalem the crowd's applause
And wide-robed celebrations cracked the tombs.
In everything, you helped him.

AGRIPPA   That is true.
He was the diplomat who reconciled
Us to our wayward Chians, to Ilium,
And when I could be angry with them, calmed,
Negotiated, led us from thunderstorm
To April daisies in the picnic grass.

CAESAR   You are a peacemaker, a wind of spring
That draws the petals through their labouring
To open hope and close suspicion's ears:
And our Messalla thanks you, now he hears
You blocked the gladiators Antony
Called from the Euxine sea for Actium.
Messalla saw to it each was destroyed;
Your capture was not wasted. Men of the sword
Died by their livelihood.

HEROD   Augustus Caesar,
Great master of the world, whose lightest breath
Storms up the desert sands and tames the waves,

I know Messalla. As I came to Rome
Along the flint blocks of the Via Latina,
Mortised to save the traveller in the dark
From tripping, we all blessed his thoughtfulness
Who used his spoils of war to smooth our steps
And save from omens and dark augury.

MESSALLA   Augustus was himself an Augur when,
Years back, he made an extra place for me
Inside the College of Augurs.

CAESAR   For your genius
In the Sicilian War.

MESSALLA   I who was least
Deserving, and had most provoked your rod.
But Caesar gazed into an enemy,
Herod, to find the friend that I became.
He made me Consul, whom he justly might
Decapitate.

CAESAR   And in return you saved
My life. Herod; you come to stand before
My judgement. Speak.

HEROD   Caesar, you gave my sons,
Alexander and Aristobulus,
The hive of empire as their honey-pot
In your own kitchen; but it spoiled them.
I am to blame. Nothing was held too dear.
My love was the full moon bathing their sea;
But the black depths hatched monsters of
          contempt,
Conspiring to eat up their source of light
And plunge Judaea in darkness. To kill me
They've plotted dusk and dawn. Hostile and
          cold,
Unloving to their father, jealous brutes
Clawing their future to control my throne,
Make my catastrophe their catapult
To supreme office under you. Poison

Is plotted. I pollute your Roman ears
With the worst crime to which loved sons can
          sink.
I, who gave Berenice, Salome's daughter,
As beautiful as is release from pain,
To Aristobulus; who gave Alexander
A princess, dark, voluptuous daughter of
King Archelaus of Cappadocia,
And all the treasure sons of mine should prize;
I ask, great Caesar, I may be revenged,
And that no sunlight peer beneath their lids
Who saw their way to what all life forbids :
Parricide.

CAESAR   Herod. Your sons are in tears.
We shall all weep if this goes on. You boys,
Whom I have loved, and Herod, your own
          father,
Brought up with silk of hope and frankincense
Of expectation: can you really wish
To pluck a crown from premature despair?
And ease with horror what your sons will fear?

ARISTOBULUS   Great Caesar; if we cannot speak it is
Not cancered conscience, rather wretchedness
That our great father, who has shown his love
By bringing us to you, known through the world
As saviour of mankind, rather than act
As punisher himself; that our own source
Should cut the veins of parenthood, and turn
His teeth where he would kiss.

ALEXANDER   The father has
All power of life and death. The king's own
          might,
Too, could have ended us. He brings us here
Where clemency is king. Would any kill
Inside a temple? This is sacred ground.

ARISTOBULUS   All princes risk the calumny that they
Nourish impatience for what will be theirs.

HEROD   Caesar, you gave me right to leave my kingdom
                 To whom among my children that I choose
                 As being most loyal and appropriate,
                 When you gave me Bashan and Gilead.

CAESAR   I did.

HEROD   And I have other sons; one older
                 By Doris the Idumaean—Antipater
                 Who never falters in his faithfulness.

CAESAR   Children, what do you say?

ALEXANDER   We ask no light
                 Linger our eyelids if suspicion breeds.
                 We mourn our mother—Caesar, who would not
                 Would be a matricide indeed! Our tears
                 For her are damp, not poisoned. If a king
                 Has sons whose mother he has put to death,
                 Nothing that they can do deflects suspicion
                 From plotting to assassinate their father.
                 If we grieve, we rebel against his will;
                 And if we're silent, we are cold, inhuman
                 Offspring. There is nothing we can ask,
                 But throw ourselves down at your feet and say
                 We have not plotted our king's judgement day.

                 ALEXANDER *kneels.*

CAESAR   Aristobulus?

ARISTOBULUS   Lord of all men, and our
                 Peacemaker, mediator; we are clean.
                 No country would allow a parricide
                 To rule. You, Caesar, would soon punish us
                 With justice unexampled. Our mother's death
                 In execution by our father is
                 A lesson to us, rather than a spur
                 To self-annihilating escapades.
                 We have committed no crime. There can be
                 Nothing to acquit. Caesar, let us lament

The slanders on our mother, not her end;
And our so fractured love help us to mend.

ARISTOBULUS *kneels.*

CAESAR   Herod, though both are cleared of the offence,
They are at fault in having so behaved
That you were forced to bring them here to me.
The gods look down on healing tears, and bless
A royal father who knows gentleness.
Embrace; be children once again as when
You climbed his knee and leaned back to the
        floor
Clasped by protecting hands, and asked for more
Time truanted from royalty for fun.
Apologize. Obey your father. Go.
Destroy suspicion. My embrace heals all.

HEROD   How can we ever thank magnificence?

CAESAR   Follow your sons. Make this a new beginning,
Suspicion's grub burst to a butterfly.
Herod; half the copper mines of Cyprus
Are yours—control the other half for me.

HEROD   I shall, and all I ever have is yours.

CAESAR   Galaesus stepped between two warring sides
To make peace, and was killed. When life
        divides
Us from each other—no more family wars!

Fade to black.

SCENE TWELVE

CAESAR *and* VIRGIL.

CAESAR   You waited. Herod has forgiven both
His cubs.

VIRGIL   Helped by your generosity?
                   A father should not linger out his life
                   Beyond his son's. Each of us has our day
                   Fixed; brief and irretrievable our time
                   For every one of us; yet we can win
                   The future by brave actions, long remembered,
                   And loving acts of generosity.

CAESAR   I'm not sure what he wants.

VIRGIL   Security?

CAESAR   Gold.

VIRGIL   Some release from nightmares.

CAESAR   That is true.
                   He sleep-cries: 'Mariammë!' Wakes in longing;
                   Lays out rare banquets for the two of them
                   In private; orders servants summon her,
                   To say that all is ready; help her dress
                   In Cleopatra's silks which, in Judaea—
                   When Herod met his bed-soft conqueror
                   And she had flirted gifts with him before
                   He led Anubis' queen back to the Nile—
                   Cleopatra draped on her client's household.

VIRGIL   Dead Mariammë's conjured to a feast
                   Of love in Cleopatra's robes, bequeathed—
                   While she was pregnant by Mark Antony—
                   To Herod? Mariammë's shade may come
                   Some dawn when red cruel skies lift the thin
                        dew,
                   Holding the Fury's torch and breathing
                        thunder!

CAESAR   The thunder gives me nightmares. Once a year
                   I hold my hand out, sitting on the pavement,
                   For coin, because of a black, warning dream.

VIRGIL   Even an innocent is visited
              When sleep flows lightly down from the stars'
                  height
              Parting the dark and mist to bring harsh
                  dreams.
              I dread them still. They take me back to when
              My health was broken by those winter storms
              Pounding the Adriatic when I followed
              Julius Caesar, and we hunted Pompey.
              Antony led the ships. One fleet was wrecked.

CAESAR   Just before you met me?

VIRGIL   Yes. I was twenty.
              A squalling gust out of the north struck right
              Across our sail, lifting waves high as night.
              The oars snapped, our prow swung round to
                  receive
              A towering precipice cascading down
              Unstoppable that, sucking, opened up
              The seething, sandy bed of the sea below.
              Three ships were flung on to a reef of rocks
              By a south blast which, to our horror,
                  mountained
              Them in sand. Some teetered on waves' crests.
              Another spun round three times in one place
              Hurling the helmsman headfirst to the storm
              Till all was swallowed by the whirlpool down.
              Our seams uncaulked, the lethal flood washed in.

CAESAR   Yet you came through the storms.

VIRGIL   Only to see
              Half-living sailors, tossed from crests of waves,
              Silenced like frost across Pharsalia.

CAESAR   And you were invalided home?

VIRGIL   We reached—
              Those who survived—the port Dyrrhachium;

Endured a winter siege of icy horror
Before the battle fought on a day so hot
Across the stifling plains of Thessaly
That harvesters could only reap at night.
If I now find it hard to sail rough seas,
Survive cold, or the summer's oven, or
Follow a victor's arms, I am not helpless.

CAESAR   You left for Naples, Epidius, and me.

VIRGIL   It was Parthenius who taught me Greek—
Yes, a freed prisoner-of-war, whose gift
Was perfect elegiacs, faultless poems.
He gathered brief love-stories, so that Gallus
Could turn them into song. Parthenius sleeps
Watched over by sea-deities, by Glaucus,
Panopea, Melícertes—Ino's son—
Beside a river graved in celandine.

CAESAR   Gallus! Your pride in status soon forgot
All power comes from the market-place.

VIRGIL   From God.
The thoughtless often say a well-run state
Can have no room for heroes, failing to see
That heroism is spiritual.

CAESAR   Virgil,
Have you a wish beyond your private hopes?
Mine is the longing to believe.

VIRGIL   Mine is
The longing to have something to believe
Beyond the appalling weight of destiny
And pity for both victor and the slain.
Anyone who has killed knows what I mean.
There must be more than this.

CAESAR   Time is the gift
We use to bring the world under one peace—
Our Pax Romana.

VIRGIL   Time is the gift indeed.
         For me it is enough that you allow
         Us to love you. How otherwise can I
         Cause love to be returned? A breeze blows on
         The night, and all the vault of heaven is starred.
         In one tent two men weep: a father mourns
         His son, yet kneels to kiss the killer's hands;
         And his son's victor, raising the broken king,
         Weeps too, for him, who looks so like his father.
         Their tears unite in a strange sympathy:
         The killer, too, had lost his closest friend.

CAESAR   It is enough that grief, and pain, have end.

         Fade.

                    SCENE THIRTEEN

              AGRIPPA *and* LIVIA.

AGRIPPA Mother of Rome, Livia, you once guided
         Augustus to make me his son-in-law,
         Lifting a peasant, plebeian puritan
         Up from a shrub to perch the morning lark.

LIVIA   Agrippa, when my husband was near death
         It was to you he gave his signet ring;
         Not to Marcellus. You were already heir
         To his *imperium.*

AGRIPPA   Only the Senate and People
         Can grant that, and it will not come to me.

LIVIA   But to your small son, Gaius!

AGRIPPA   Sometimes I dread
         History repeating like a water-wheel.
         That rivalry, that wounded all our world
         So long, forking its double tongue

Through Antony and our Octavian,
Might split the oak of state between new blows
By your first son, Tiberius, and my
Julia's Gaius; and, when your sacred falcon
Riding the air from a high crag, stoops on
Our dove in a far cloud, catches and grips
To scoop out entrails with the scything claws
While blood and feathers waft down from the
     sky,
We shall no longer be on earth to mourn.

LIVIA

You're not an augur—that's no prophecy.
What I shall tell you now is true. Years back,
When you were cutting channels to the sea,
Opening the Lucrine lake to ships, a pure
White sea-bird carrying a laurel-sprig
With berries was thrown by a sudden eagle
Into my lap. Octavian wanted me.
We had just met. Warm feathers from the sky
Shocked and delighted me. I nurtured it
Between my breasts, planted those laurel berries
Whose leaves surround the brows of men like
     you,
In triumph, now.

AGRIPPA

              Yes; you were destined to
Hold to your heart the pure gift of the heavens,
Son of a god, whose laurels are your care.

LIVIA

The pure gift of the heavens does test my hold!
He brought Terentia, that slight child-bride,
Unclothed before us at an evening meal,
And made me strip beside her, both parade
Before our guests in a contest of beauty.

AGRIPPA

I'm sure you won.

LIVIA

              I did. She was naive.
What is a shivering embarrassment
To echoing years of lonely solitude?

AGRIPPA   How strange you married him who exiled you
With small Tiberius, before he knew
Your beauty's violet.

LIVIA   You need not fear.
Gaius succeeds Augustus—who is here.

SCENE FOURTEEN

Enter CAESAR.

CAESAR   Agrippa, perfect colleague. Your small daughter
By Attica, your first wife: might you not
Graft her stem to bud by Tiberius?

AGRIPPA   Vipsania? Marry Tiberius
Your step-son?

LIVIA   Yes; we're speaking of my boy.

AGRIPPA   Vipsania's too young!

CAESAR   Tiberius likes her.
She's granddaughter of Cicero's best friend.
Marriage would channel past and future hates
To river-nesting swans of healed content.

LIVIA   Why are you silent?

AGRIPPA   I had not thought so great an honour was
So near to one so small. She is my dream
Of hope beyond the grave, my future's means
Of fond remembrance; my first leap of faith.

CAESAR   Then take it. I, too, hope beyond the grave—
That men will say I gave Rome best of all
Government, constitution; everlasting
Foundations that will leave the state secure
To weather every storm new years may gust

Unshaken. That will be my one reward
For single-minded service, the dawn lamp
Of sleepless duty, and the high demands
Imposed on loving friends. Messalla! Come!

SCENE FIFTEEN

Enter MESSALLA.

CAESAR   Have you prepared to take the auspices
I asked? You know the will of the gods?

MESSALLA   I do,
Caesar Augustus. Yes. The sacred fowl
Received their food.

AGRIPPA   Those chickens pecked
    their corn?
Why do you take such trivia seriously?
'They're eating now!' 'Silence must reign!'
    'Some sacred
Crumb falls from the beak.' We would eat fast
If cooped and starved, then stared at.

MESSALLA   You prefer
Divination from entrails?

AGRIPPA   We used to watch
The heavens; now stare down at a poulter's
    block.
No Roman augur will presume to read
The mind of Jupiter from flights of birds,
The eagle's skill; no. He peers into guts
('A cleft in the liver is financial gain')
To see which liver is without a 'head'.
What if the next hot liver reassures
Because it has one? Which has precedence?
Ye gods! I'd sooner throw a soldier's dice.
They're clean, and do not smell.

MESSALLA   It is not what we do but who we are,
            Agrippa. We advise the Senate, like
            Our rival College of Pontiffs. Only we,
            The Augurs, we—true bridge from gods to
                men—
            May interrupt assemblies, have the power
            To prove ill-omens force the frown of heaven.

CAESAR   Useful authority; and that's why we
            Choose carefully the College of Augurs,
            And keep their number small.

MESSALLA   But even we
            May not disturb the Senate; that's supreme:
            True mediating door to the divine.
            Priests are its servants.

AGRIPPA   Same old politics.
            My Pantheon will be a butcher's shop.
            When Augurs meet how can they stifle laughs?
            Ah well! It keeps the masses on their knees.
            Caesar, I'll leave to obey crawling cheese.

            Exit AGRIPPA.

MESSALLA   Why so upset?

CAESAR   Our new idea disturbs
            His family. All will be well; you'll see.
            He has nowhere to go. He must agree.

            Exeunt.

SCENE SIXTEEN

PROPERTIUS *and* TERENTIA.

PROPERTIUS   Horace has sung your praises in a poem.

TERENTIA   Venus! How did you get it? Let me hear—
Only if there's no malice in it!

PROPERTIUS   Horace?
No malice? It's to your husband, Maecenas.
It shirks the duty of a praise of Rome.
'My buzzing Muse inspires me to sing a beauty's
   praise—
Your honeyed, light-eyed, lissom Terentia's
   loving gaze.
See how she drops decorum and steps out to
   the dance,
And gracefully takes up each hand with smiling
   nonchalance
Exchanging gentle banter with perfect steps
   and turns!
Who would lose one lock of her hair for all
   Arabia burns?
Her neck twists up to kiss you; as you bend,
   turns away,
Teasing from you in earnest shared pleasure's
   holiday.'

TERENTIA   (*Clapping*) Did Horace really write that? The
feet sound more like yours.

PROPERTIUS   The words are his. My music has gone grey.

TERENTIA   Propertius, why? Mourning for Cynthia?

PROPERTIUS   The funeral fire licked round those limbs I
   loved,
But the pale ghost's escaped! I could not sleep,

Moaning the frigid empire of my bed;
Then I saw peering over me her eyes,
Her hair, both just as at the funeral;
The dress scorched down one side. Burning had
          bitten
The beryl from her ring. Lethe had washed
Her lips white, but the voice was just the same.

TERENTIA   Did Cynthia speak?

PROPERTIUS   Her brittle knuckles cracked,
But not her spirit: 'Liar! Girl-betrayer!
How can you sleep so soon? Have you forgotten
Our window-escapades and love-making?
Our promises—blown by unlistening wind!
When darkness closed my eyes, not one voice
          spoke
My name. You could have saved me one more
          day.
My head was propped up on a broken tile,
Gashed. Were you there in black, weeping my
          bier?
If you could not accompany my corpse
Beyond the gates, you might have slowed it
          down;
Prayed the winds fan my flames, burned scented
          spice.
Was it beyond your purse to buy cheap flowers
To throw on me, or break a jar of wine
Across my ashes? Torture Lygdamus,
That slave, with white-hot iron. I drank his wine
And know that drained me pale. Your mincing
          whore,
Who sold herself in public for cheap nights
Just yesterday, now trails a gilt-edged robe,
In mud. Old Petalë, who flowered my grave,
She punishes, chains to a filthy log;
And Lalagë, who used my name to ask
A favour's hung up from her twisted hair
By her, and flogged.'

TERENTIA   Is that the woman who
                 Melted down Cynthia's statue for its gold,
                 Called it her dowry?

PROPERTIUS   Yes, she runs my house.
                 Cynthia's ghost still glared. 'I will not scold,
                 Though you deserve it. I was for years the
                     queen
                 Of your verse. I swear I kept faith. If not,
                 May hissing vipers slime round my remains!
                 I do not tell the underworld of your
                 Innumerable infidelities,
                 But ask you this . Don't let my loyal maid
                 Hold up a looking-glass to a new mistress.
                 Burn all our poems. Tend ivy on my grave
                 Whose swelling tendrils feel my delicate bones;
                 And on a pillar write my epitaph.
                 Though other women now possess you, soon
                 I alone shall entwine you, bone in bone.'
                 Then she was gone; and I clasped airy mist.

TERENTIA   I've never feared the ferryman till now,
                 Nor sleepy darkness. Let me wipe your brow.

                 Exeunt.

                           SCENE SEVENTEEN

                      CAESAR *and* JULIA.

CAESAR   Julia. My daughter. Come here. Why are you
                     scratching?

JULIA   I have a boil.

CAESAR   Why?

JULIA   Why does anyone?

CAESAR   Because of unhealthy living. You are my boil,
              My tumour I must cut out.

JULIA   Father, Phoebe,
              My freedwoman, rather than face you now,
              Last night hanged herself.

CAESAR   She knew her shame.
              I wish I'd been her father and not yours.
              I helped you to read Homer. Here's a line:
              'Would I had not once married, and I had died
                    without children!'

JULIA   Father, what can I do or say to please you?
              Your youth was sultry. I am yours.

CAESAR   In the Forum,
              Up on the very Rostra where I had
              Announced the new laws that would purify
              Rome's morals, you danced with your drunken
                    guests,
              Lay down in front of all, and welcomed in
              Iulus Antonius, Antony's son!

JULIA   I kept my dress on.

CAESAR   In flagrant debauch.
              Iulus Antonius, whom I had spared,
              Lifted into the priesthood, made a Praetor,
              Even allowed to marry my sister's daughter!
              You chose public adultery with him.
              He's killed himself.

JULIA   He's dead! Oh gods!

CAESAR   Yes; cold.
              Each, every detail has come back to me,
              And I have written a full letter to
              The Senate, which is being read out by
              A Quaestor, now, as I see you.

JULIA   What hope
Have I?

CAESAR   Plenty. You are banished to
An island off Campania for life.
Never again will you drink wine. No male,
Slave or free may approach unless I know
His age, height, name, complexion, birthmarks,
        scars
And have granted exceptional permission.
As for your other lovers, 'austere' Crispinus,
Prattling Sempronius Gracchus, Claudius
        Pulcher,
Cornelius Scipio—nobles! (God knows who else
Down to the meanest slave you fornicate)
They will be dealt with, one by one. Not death.
I'll set a date to limit accusations
Against you and your girls. I can be kind;
But you will never see my face again.

Fade to black.

                        SCENE EIGHTEEN

                LIVIA *and* HORACE.

LIVIA   Herod's strangled his sons.

HORACE   What did Augustus
Say?

LIVIA   Only that for their trial this time
Roman officials attend and all take place
Away from Herod's kingdom—in Beirut.
You know Augustus is abroad, inspecting
The sunrise kingdoms and the isles of Greece.
In Athens he met Virgil; now both sail
Together, homeward, on the Adriatic.
Please will you say a prayer for safe return?

Crowd forms to welcome the fleet.

HORACE   *In front of the crowd on the harbour.*

May Venus, goddess of the Cyprus shore,
With the twin brothers of Troy's Helen, guiding,
And Aeolus, who holds the winds from war,
Blowing from east-south-east in sails swift
          gliding,
So cherish and preserve our ship of Rome
That Virgil, brother of my soul, reach home.

The man who first committed a frail boat
Into the furious sea, unknowing, trusting,
Must have enclosed his heart, to stay afloat,
In oak and triple brass. Sirocco gusting
Into pugnacious northern blasts, dry-eyed
He faced, and monsters, rocks, storms he
          defied.

Caesar, our Father, may no whirlwind seize
You from us for our sins. Man's restless striving
For all beyond his reach, to leap the seas
Estranging coast from coast, dares God's
          conniving.
Fire snatched from heaven, hell raped, false
          wings through air—
Our crimes claw thunderbolts that Jove would
          spare.

CAESAR *and* VIRGIL.

CAESAR   You heard the shouts that welcomed us on
                    shore,
               Watched the red, practised banners, lifted high,

Slowly lower in unison their points
Reflecting in the bay the setting sun?

VIRGIL   The sickness of the waves, my jolting litter,
The fumes and smells of fish and rigging, wine
From last night's celebration on the ram-
Prowed quinquereme following your purple sails,
Have made me weak, so that I'm half-aware
Of Caesar's glory on the harbour quay
For our homecoming to Brundisium.

CAESAR   Tonight you rest; and when we leave tomorrow
Along the Appian Way for cheering Rome,
You must remain in this salt air until
The dust of Athens, heat of Megara,
That gave you sunstroke and this shaking fever,
Are stilled by dittany from Crete, that draws
The arrow poison from the body's quiver.

VIRGIL   Caesar, I've made my will. You, who made me
When I came to you begging father's farm,
Accept my whole life's gratitude, and love,
As I lie here beside the darkening sea.
One quarter of all that I have is yours.

CAESAR   Your love is precious. Never have you lied
Or failed me since—years back—we smiled in
        class
At old Epidius. Remember?

VIRGIL   Yes.
I only wish all that you say were true.

CAESAR   You brought me warning once, and saved my
        life.
Perhaps with convalescence you can work
On last revisions of your *Aeneid*.
Have you some section I can take with me?
Those night words for our lost Marcellus?

VIRGIL   Caesar,

My epic is the lie. It's not my fever
That makes me ache to burn it in the flames.

CAESAR   Burn your life's masterpiece? Posterity's
Mirror of all the best that we've achieved?
No! That would be the final degradation
Betraying all God's creativity.

VIRGIL   But don't you see? The poem is the shell.
Yours has been the achievement, moulding a
          new
World-system that will last two thousand years,
Our night of horror ended. Man of Rome,
Do not forget to rule the nations. These
Will be your arts: to impose settled peace,
Spare the defeated, and cut down the proud.

CAESAR   'The toga'd Romans, rulers of the earth',
As you have called us. How could you destroy
Embodiment of our ideals?

VIRGIL   Ideals
Become idolatry when ends are used
To justify the means to them. To look
Deeply into the truth of all creation
(Lucretius in his poem showed us how)
Is to withdraw from writing for the State;
To live ideals, try to embody them,
Not beautify the compromising lie.

CAESAR   The truth! The truth! What is the truth?
          Sometimes
Decisions must be taken, even if wrong,
If rulers are to ride chaotic tides
And sail those trusting in them to the shore.

VIRGIL   No! Not in heart-wrung poems that ring true.
All things must die, and that includes the arts,
And beauty's monuments we hold so dear,
Except the truth—in any form it's found;
A million times a day quite unperceived.

CAESAR   Can a great ruler be a good man?

VIRGIL   No.
              We pay him highly as we buy his soul
              To do for us the things we would not do.
              A man of goodness will be one who suffers.
              What rule he has is by example, as
              We learn when loved ones die. What time distils
              Is what was true; and that truth grows from love.

CAESAR   How can love rule the world?

VIRGIL   The one salvation
              For the defeated is to have no hope
              They will be saved.

CAESAR   The slave's mentality!
              The degradation of complete despair.

VIRGIL   That is the wistfulness of our strange world,
              Atoms compounded by Necessity
              That climb from olive branches wreathed in wool
              Through the bees' discipline and loyalties
              To heartbreak Orpheus suffered as he turned
              Too soon, and looking back lost all he loved.

CAESAR   Heroic bees, for me, that swarm in order,
              Die in their work, yet still the race goes on.

VIRGIL   A tiny handful of dust puts them to rest.
              Orpheus was torn to pieces, but his head,
              Washed down the river Hebrus, still cried out:
              'Eurydice!' Love conquers even death.

              VIRGIL *dies.*

CAESAR   So this is immortality! My brother,
              Will anything bring joy to me again
              Without you? It's the dawn. What can light bring
              For misery of human suffering?

END OF ACT TWO

Epilogue

He did not come from noble blood.
    Born in a roadside ditch,
His mother, Maia, saw there stood
A poplar tree where babyhood
Began. His father understood
    Bees; neither poor nor rich.

And yet this child of streams became
    The grave voice of our race.
The modest master overcame
Diffidence, war-pride, frightening fame
To be the conscience of Rome's name,
    Save Empire from disgrace.

He saw what new times might fulfil;
    Dead souls, by Sibyl's charms;
Like leaves that fall in autumn's chill
Or flocked birds winging south until
They reach far sunnier shores, these still
    Stretch out their longing arms.

A poet's shade too soon rests here—
    Unjust skies could not wait—
Skilled as the greatest minds there were
In Athens: Rome could challenge her
In him; but there's no vanquisher
    Of adamantine Fate.

FINIS

An Epic Completed

Keith Critchlow*'s review of* Virgil and Caesar.

THE STAGE, 5.iii.1992

In his new play, *Virgil and Caesar*, the completion of a serial epic entitled AGORA, Francis Warner explores the dramatic tension between worldly rule, the pragmatism of politics, and the vision of the poet as idealist.

Staged in the uniquely fitting setting of Oxford University's Convocation House, the production by Tim Prentki and Dominic Shellard exploited the limited space of extraordinary fan-vaulted beauty to fine advantage.

The play, as it explored the relationships between machinations of worldly power, the wooing of the army, the detecting of subterfuge from the judiciary, the temptation of tyrannical power, the duties of family life, and the seductive disasters of succumbing to lust, unfolded in masterly fashion against the background of the philosophical and other views of the poets.

Caesar Augustus, Agrippa his General, and Maecenas his adviser try to keep up with the mood of the 'god' ruler whilst Murena plots against him. The poets Propertius, Horace and Virgil represent different aspects of the position of poet as participator and commentator. Virgil, 'whitest of men', being the 'longest-lasting, loyalest friend' of Caesar, dutifully advises, and thereby represents the conscience of any pragmatist, whether god, king or politician.

Warner brings to our attention the perennial conflicts that are as timeless as they are timely. The command of English through poetic imagery must rank as the very best. Here we have laid before us the perennial crises of humanity dressed in classical clothes yet intensely of today.

The Caesar of Daniel Williams, and the Virgil of Mark Payton, were intimations of two young actors we are bound to hear more of. Both Julius D'Silva as Horace and Jason Tann as Herod demonstrated the power of dramatic delivery. However, the show was nearly stolen by the three girls: Sophie Paul as the dignified wife of Caesar, Alice

Kennedy as the ravishing and much ravished daughter of Caesar, and Susanna Kane, whose moving performance as the wife of Maecenas, Caesar's adviser, was all the more highlighted by the fact that she is only 15 years old.

How valuable such rare and important plays are, being written in times when not only biological species are under threat around the world, but also cultural continuity itself.

Imperious Caesar

Review by Jasper Griffin *of Balliol College,*
Professor of Classical Literature, and
Public Orator of the University of Oxford.

OXFORD MAGAZINE, 9.iii.1992

Francis Warner has a long connection with Oxford theatre. His early period was marked by the spectacular. . . His middle period, through which we are now living, is gentler and more didactic. A series of poetic dramas has brought on stage the Florence of Botticelli and Savonarola, the Rome of Nero and Seneca, Justinian's Byzantium, and the Athens of Pericles. This latest play deals with the Rome of (Augustus) Caesar and his dealings with the Augustan poets.

The plays are written in verse, essentially decasyllabic, the scenes often closed with a rhyming couplet:

> Stay with me while I sleep, and trim the light.
> Your thoughts, weightless as wind, will calm my night.

That conservatism of form goes with a diction which is classicising, at times consciously noble, even beautiful. Such a style can become self-indulgent. Warner is careful to keep it in bounds, as in Caesar's monologues on his great rival, whose memory continues to haunt the mind of the victor.

Another risk for the poet has clearly been his detailed knowledge of the period. At moments the audience could have been spared some information (Agrippa's aqueducts, Messalla's repair of the Via Latina, the procedure of the Senate), which in the first half of the play can impede the action; but the second half runs with convincing dramatic power. And it must be said that Warner's details are pretty accurate, in a period in which—not to speak of Shakespeare making a clock strike in his *Julius Caesar*—many writers of high scholarly pretensions have opened themselves to the exultant jeers of the professionals.

Pericles, Seneca, Justinian, the early Medici: common to all these plays is the focusing on a moment in history when the attempt was made to ennoble the life of man, to produce that great society, radiant in arts and civilised in politics, which is the mirage that haunts the traveller through the dusty plains of human history. Choice spirits struggle to unite beauty, justice, peace. Of course the struggle is always lost in the end: violence, bigotry, stinginess, and philistinism, the four horsemen whose horses can always be heard—at best—trampling outside the stockade, ride in triumph over it at last,

> And gone are Phidias' famous ivories
> And all the golden grasshoppers and bees.[1]

In this play it is the disintegration of the family which marks the coming of the rot; Herod kills his sons, Caesar denounces and banishes his unchaste daughter; Maecenas' brother-in-law must be condemned for treason.

Virgil and Caesar has as its centre the relationship of the Emperor and his greatest poet. Warner follows the *Lives* of Virgil produced in late antiquity, which present him as having been at school with Augustus, and as a life-long friend. As Virgil was six or seven years older, that is perhaps less accurate history than pleasing invention; biographers resemble nature, if in nothing else, in abhorring a vacuum. But the existence of the ancient documents does license the playwright in his conception. Propertius, a romantic and unpolitical poet, and Horace, an urbane and malicious one, recite their own poems. Warner is very deft at working them in, and some fine effects are achieved; as when Horace recites his ode addressed to Virgil (*Odes* 1.3) as a prayer for his friend's safe homecoming from what proves to be his last journey, or Propertius recites to Julia his poem about the ghost of his dead Cynthia returning to threaten and reproach him (Prop. 4.7). And the symposium of poets with Maecenas, all drinking and jostling in their different styles, is delicious.

But between Caesar and Virgil things are more serious. Caesar, who has been insistently anxious for the *Aeneid*, is distracted by the arrival of King Herod, asking for permission to strangle his sons ('I'd rather be Herod's pig than Herod's son!' comments the Emperor) and interrupts the poet's lyrical account of his plans for the longed-for poem with a preoccupied

> Acceptable. King Herod and his sons
> Wait for me . . .

[1] W. B. Yeats's poem 'Nineteen Hundred and Nineteen', lines 7 & 8.

The Emperor tries conscientiously to learn from the wisdom and gentleness of Virgil. His own quick temper causes the death of Virgil's friend, the poet Gallus, against his own will; like Antony, Gallus was unbalanced by Egypt, the opposite pole to Rome. Virgil cannot write plain patriotic paeans; but he does not simply turn away from the world of action, violence, and inevitable guilt. In the moving scene of Virgil's death, which ends the play, Caesar asks 'Can a great ruler be a good man?'

Virgil replies,

> No.
> We pay him highly as we buy his soul
> To do for us the things we would not do . . .

But Virgil also tells the Emperor that he would like to burn his own unfinished epic, perceiving the world of action as the more real.

Warner has had his plays produced in some of Oxford's most splendid buildings, the Sheldonian, the University Church, and Convocation House; the noble settings suit his aspiring verse. He has also appeared, less magnificently but still imposingly, in the Examination Schools; and even, by one of the longest aesthetic leaps imaginable, in the Newman Rooms. Convocation House turns out to be a delightful little theatre, although its seats are not for weaklings or Sybarites—definitely Rome, not Egypt.

The cast, by and large, did well. The women were good; Virgil spoke and looked just right; Herod was engagingly sinister and Levantine. Warner's verse, well spoken by most of the cast, filled the ear satisfyingly, and echoes in the memory. The end of every human life is death; the works of human minds, artist or scholar or statesman, do not endure for ever. Yet in history, not once but many times, the attempt has been made to realise the ideal, to produce a society radiant and ennobled. Augustus and Virgil had such a vision, however incomplete or inadequate its execution. It would be nice to think that in our own forthcoming election our leaders were at least trying to emulate them.